Astrology

Cherry Gilchrist

Batsford Academic and Educational Ltd   London

© Cherry Gilchrist 1982
First published 1982
All rights reserved. No part of this publication may be reproduced, in any form or by any means, without permission from the Publisher

Typeset by DP Press, Sevenoaks
and printed in Great Britain by
R.J. Acford,
Chichester, Sussex
for the publishers
Batsford Academic and Educational Ltd,
an imprint of B T Batsford Ltd,
4 Fitzhardinge Street
London W1H 0AH

ISBN 0 7134 3543 7

ACKNOWLEDGMENT

The Author and Publishers would like to thank the following for their kind permission to reproduce copyright illustrations: Mrs Pam Bennett, fig 57; The Bodleian Library, figs 5, 24, 25; The Trustees of the British Museum, figs 11, 12; The Mansell Collection Ltd, figs 10, 13, 16, 17, 19, 20, 23, 26, 29, 30, 31, 38, 41, 49; Zach Matthews, figs 56, 58, 59; The National Portrait Gallery, figs 48, 53; The University Library, Cambridge, figs 6, 7, 8, 22, 33, 35, 37, 39, 40, 42, 44, 51, 54. Figs 14, 15, 18, 60 are copyright of the Author. All other illustrations are from the Publishers' collection. Figs 1, 2, 9, 27, 28 and 36 were drawn by Jane Oldfield.

Contents

Acknowledgment — 2

List of Illustrations — 4

1. What is Astrology? — 5
2. The Earliest Astrologers — 13
3. Magic and Medicine — Astrology in Medieval England — 20
4. Astrology in England, 1450-1700 — Food for Philosophers, Priests and Poets — 29
5. Predictions for the People, 1450-1700 — 39
6. Astrology at Low Ebb, 1700-1850 — 48
7. The Road Leads On — Astrology from 1850 to the Present Day — 56

Date List — 66

Glossary — 68

Books for Further Reading — 70

Index — 71

List of Illustrations

1	The signs of the zodiac	6
2	The ecliptic	7
3	Aries the ram	8
4	Women and the moon	8
5	Mercury	9
6	Saturn	9
7	Virgo	10
8	Aquarius	11
9	Planetary aspects	12
10	Great Ziggurat of Ur	13
11	Babylonian boundary stone	14
12	Assyrian astrological instrument	15
13	The goddess Nut	15
14	Ram-headed sphinxes	16
15	The Great Pyramid, Giza	16
16	Hipparchus	17
17	Roman amulet	19
18	Standing stones	20
19	Albumazar	21
20	Halley's comet	22
21	The Four Humours	23
22	The zodiac and parts of the body	24
23	The zodiac and parts of the face	25
24	Correspondences	26
25	*The Complaint of Mars and Venus*	27
26	An astrolabe	28
27	Ptolomaic system	30
28	Copernican system	30
29	Beyond the stars	31
30	Measuring the sun's angle	32
31	Sixteenth-century astronomer	33
32	Dante's *Inferno*	34
33	Jupiter and Mars	35
34	Jupiter	36
35	The horoscope of a comet	37
36	The planets and the human body	38
37	William Lilly	40
38	John Evans	41
39	An eclipse	43
40	Sagittarius	44
41	From the *Shepherd's Calendar*	45
42	Almanack page	46
43	Lilly and the Great Fire	47
44	"Poor Robin" almanack	47
45	A fraudulent astrologer	49
46	Ebenezer Sibly	50
47	America's declaration of Independence	50
48	Sir William Herschel	51
49	Herschel discovers Uranus	52
50	*The Astrologer of the Nineteenth Century*	53
51	The death of Lord Byron	54
52	Zadkiel's magazine	55
53	Richard Garnett	56
54	*The Astrologer*	58
55	Alan Leo	60
56	Charles Carter	61
57	Astrological Conference programme	62
58	A group of people with Capricorn ascendant	63
59	John Addey	64
60	A modern horoscope	65

1
What is Astrology?

Man is a questioner. As far back as we can trace his history, he has always tried to discover more about the world around him. What is it made of? How does it work, and what can he construct from it to help him hunt, farm, and live better? What are the sun, moon, and stars, and how do they relate to us? The quest has been with us for thousands of years to learn more about ourselves and our place in the universe.

Astrology is an ancient system which uses the positions of the planets in the sky to reveal knowledge about men and their activities. It may also yield information and clues about the past and future, as well as the present. The astrologer draws up a chart called a "horoscope", which maps the planetary patterns in the sky for the moment of a man's birth. He will interpret this according to astrological tradition, and will then be able to say what type of character the man has, whether he is gentle or aggressive, for instance, whether he prefers adventure or a quiet life, the kind of work he has a talent for, and many other details about his life and personality. With further calculations, the astrologer can then consider the man's future and point to certain important times that will come in his life, describing the kind of events and changes that are likely to happen then.

In order to understand why astrology has been held in such great esteem by such large numbers of people, both in past centuries, and even in our own "scientific" twentieth century, we must try to see the world from a particular point of view. The astrologer might explain his outlook like this: "Although astrology is not a religion, most astrologers acknowledge that the world was brought into being by one creator, God. The world He created is one harmonious whole. We are part of it, as are the stars and planets in the sky above. Everything in the world is connected and ordered, everything has significance if only we can interpret it. If we know how, we can look to the patterns around us to tell us more about ourselves and the world we live in. Astrology takes the patterns of the planets in the sky, and says that these have a meaning for us."

Many astrologers have quoted the words from Genesis: "And God said, Let there be lights in the firmament of the heaven to divide the day from the night; and let them be for signs, and for seasons, and for days, and years." Philosophers and astrologers have long thought of man himself as a universe in miniature. "Heaven is man, and man is heaven, and all men together are the one heaven," said Paracelsus, a great doctor and a wise astrologer, who was born in Switzerland in 1493.

Trying to follow astrology in history, and in the writings of poets and philosophers, is far more interesting if you have a grasp

SIGNS OF THE ZODIAC AND THEIR PLANETARY RULERS

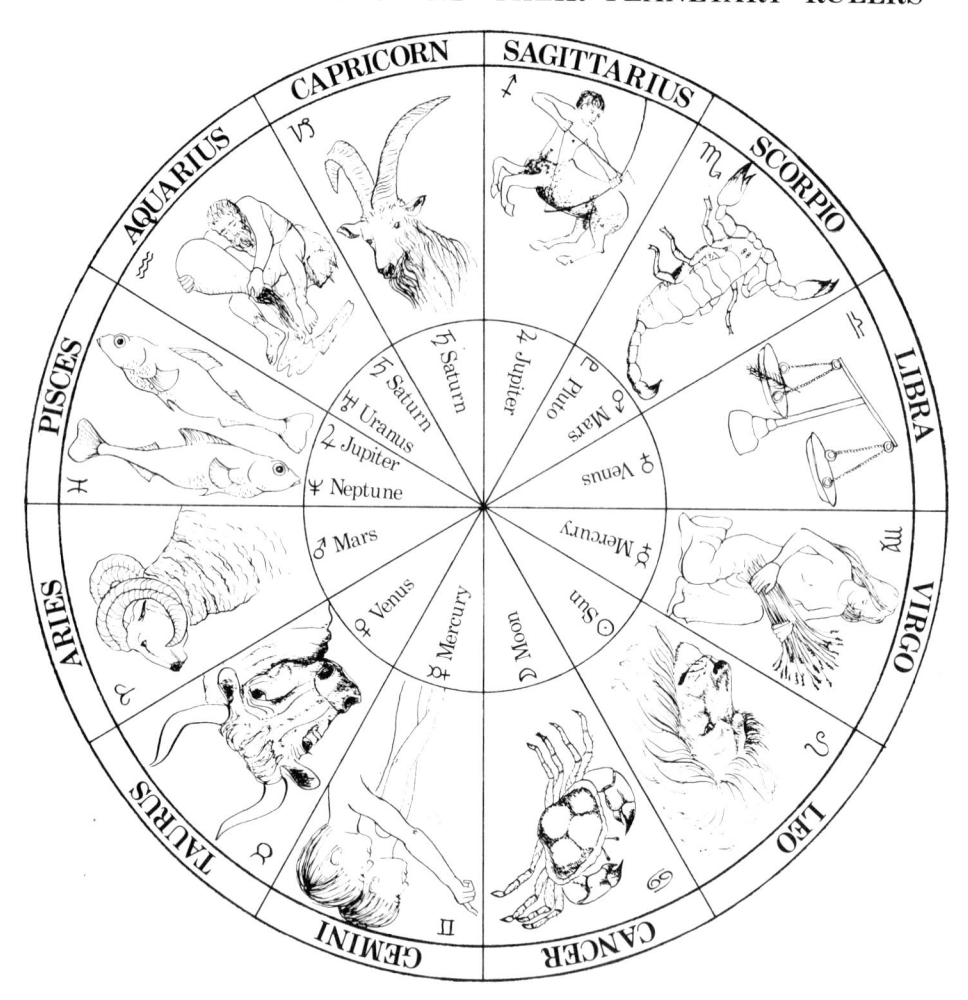

▲
1   The signs of the zodiac. Each sign is said to be ruled by one or two planets; the planetary rulers are shown on the inner wheel. The symbols for each planet and sign are also given.

of the basic symbols of the horoscope. The section which follows aims to give some of this essential information, although only a very broad outline is possible in such a short space. Drawing up a horoscope and interpreting it requires a great deal more information, study and practice, but the description here will show you how the astrologer goes about his work, and what he looks for in a horoscope. If you are interested in learning more about astrology, there are many good books available nowadays, and you will find some references to these at the end of this book.

The Physical Framework

The horoscope is basically a diagrammatic picture of the positions of the planets in the sky, as viewed from earth. "Planets", actually, is a kind of astrologer's shorthand for the true planets plus the sun and moon. A map of the heavens is drawn up for a particular moment that is thought to be significant. The most common time of significance, obviously, is the time of a birth, when a baby takes its first breath or cry. But other times, such as those for the founding of a nation, or the start of a journey, can also be used, and the chart then drawn up will give indications about the character and future of the nation, or the progress of the journey.

Most people have heard of the zodiac, and it is helpful to have an idea of what this is in physical terms. Our solar system consists of the sun at the centre, and nine known planets orbiting around it. Additionally, the moon, a satellite of the earth, plays an important part in astrology. The solar system is a plane: all the planets lie on a level with each other, like marbles on a plate. Each planet orbits at a different rate and distance from the sun. It is important to remember that, in astrology, we are concerned with how the planets appear to move *as seen from earth*. Their positions and speed of orbit would appear differently if viewed from the sun itself.

Because the solar system is a plane, all the planetary orbits can be plotted against the same background, which is a great starry circle. It is around this starry circle, called the "ecliptic" in astronomy, and the "zodiac" in astrology, that all the planets travel. Astrology divides the circle up into twelve equal sectors, each of which is named, the first being Aries, and these form the signs of the zodiac. A planet is always "in" one of these signs, and it will gradually pass through them all in order. Planets take different times to complete this zodiac cycle — the moon only one month, the time it takes, in fact, to circle the earth, and Pluto about 248 years! Even the sun appears to travel around the zodiac in the space of a year, because of the earth's own path around the sun. The earth does not "stand up straight" in its orbit, but is tilted at an angle to the plane of the solar system. This is why we have varying seasons and different hours of daylight throughout the year. For half the year the northern hemisphere is tilted towards the sun, giving summer, and for the other half it leans away from the sun, and winter results. The sun rises later and does not climb so high in the sky.

Although the planets move in regular cycles, they are always found in a combined pattern that is quite unique overall. Each horoscope is different for every moment in time. Even the same time, but a different birthplace, will produce a different chart. This is because, due to the earth's rotation on its own axis once a day, the sun and planets and the zodiac appear to rise and set each day. This means that every day each sign of the zodiac in turn seems to rise above the horizon, "culminate", or reach its highest point in the sky, and then set. But which sign is rising or setting at any one time will depend on where you are located on earth, as different horizons will give a different picture, just as the time of sunrise or sunset depends on the place from which you observe it. In astrology, the "rising sign" or "ascendant", as it is also known, is very important, and is said to show a person's outward appearance and behaviour. The culminating sign, too, is important; it is known as the "Midheaven" and indicates whether a person will attain any standing in the eyes of the world.

Nowadays, the astrologer can complete calculations with the aid of a set of tables, called an ephemeris. The positions of the

ANGLE BETWEEN THE EARTH
AND THE ECLIPTIC

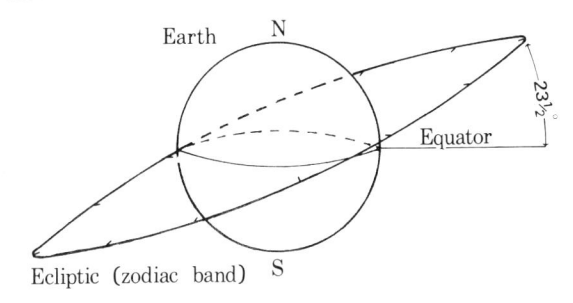

▲
2 The ecliptic is an extension into space of the plane of the solar system. Here we can see that the earth's axis is tilted at an angle to it. (Not to scale.)

▲
3 Here is an exaggerated representation from a seventeenth-century Italian book, of the similarity said to exist between a ram, and the person who has Aries ascending in his horoscope!

planets for the time in question always need to be checked, because although the length of each planetary cycle is regular, the amount each planet moves from day to day varies during the cycle. It is rather as if you set out for a walk around the block and allowed yourself five minutes to do it. If you behaved like a typical planet, you would not walk at a steady pace, but would rush forward, then slow down, then stand still, and then even walk backwards! After this, you would have to speed up again to catch up on your time schedule. When a planet appears to go backwards, we call this "retrograde motion". It appears to be retrograde because of the difference in the speeds of orbit between the planet and the earth itself.

The Interpretation of a Horoscope

Although astrology has been practised for well over 2,000 years, the rules for interpretation remain basically unchanged. Here are the basic meanings for the planets and the signs in a horoscope:

Planets — These are the "building blocks" of the psyche of man, and represent all our basic drives, instincts, faculties and values.
The Sun — Very important in the chart, the position of the sun shows the kind of person one is at heart. It also represents the father, and authority.
The Moon — Personality, habits, imagination. Shows the kind of life-style preferred. Also represents the mother, and women in general.
Mercury — This relates to communication — by speech or gesture — and also to study and writing.
Venus — Signifies our relationships with other people. Rules art and beauty, love and marriage.
Mars — Action and ambition. Mars shows the quality of our energy, and the "fighting spirit". It rules warfare.
Jupiter — Faith in life, luck, wealth. Shows how people will try to better themselves. Governs religious matters too.

◀4 A seventeenth-century engraving showing the moon's rays affecting the minds of women. The moon is said to have an especial affinity with women. As the moon waxes and wanes, so does a woman change state physically in her monthly cycle and when she bears children. In the horoscope, the moon represents, among other things, the feminine qualities and motherhood.

Saturn — In the horoscope it will show where a person's limitations lie, and where frustration and hindrance in life will occur. But it also shows the serious side of the nature, and any qualities of practicality and reliability.

The last three planets were not known to the first astrologers, but modern astrologers do use them in horoscopes and have assigned meanings to them:

Uranus — Rules the dramatic and the unexpected. Shows strength of will, and tendencies towards unconventional behaviour. Also connected with science, and with things that are either very ancient or very modern.

Neptune — The mystical and spiritual side of man's nature. Rules music and poetry and can also betoken illusion and deception.

Pluto — This will indicate potential for destruction and creation, and show whether someone can cope with crisis. Also rules death and transformation.

These three outer planets are said to relate less to the individual, and more to humanity as a whole, as they take a long time to pass through each sign of the zodiac.

5 An illustration to a fifteenth-century manuscript, showing Mercury and the kind of occupations that he rules. Writing, clockmending, organ-playing and craft work are all there.

6 A sixteenth-century woodcut of Saturn — shown with the sickle of Time in his hand.

The Signs

Zodiac is a Greek word, meaning "circle of animals", and it is amusing to note that many of the signs are symbolized by animal forms. Astrologers have always used these symbols to gain more insight into a person's type. Many people think of themselves as "a Piscean", "a Leo", and so on; this denotes the sign the sun was in at the time of birth, and is a good indication of our basic character type, although in a complete horoscope all the other planets and their placings are taken into account too. If you know someone who was born when the sun was in Cancer, for instance, ask yourself if he or she is "hard without and soft within", like a Crab, that is, defensive and prickly on the surface but soft-hearted underneath. Perhaps he or she likes to be evasive, going sideways at things, or is influenced by moods, as the crab responds to the tides, and is even, maybe, sometimes a little "crabby" in temper!

Here are the basic meanings of the signs. Each is said to be ruled by a particular planet; that is to say, each sign has an affinity with a planet. Some have double rulerships, to accommodate the outer planets discovered in recent centuries. Every sign, too, is related to one of the four

7 Virgo – a woodcut from a sixteenth-century astrological manual, written so that the reader may "find the fatal destiny, constellation, complexion, and natural inclination of every man and child by his birth". It describes one of the characteristics of Virgo thus: "He is naturally inclined to have curled hair, and red, and by nature loveth the same, in so much that if he have not such hair of that colour, yet he will seek to have the same coloured by art . . . ".
▼

elements, earth, water, fire and air. In general, the earth signs are practical, the water signs emotional, the fire signs adventurous, and the air signs intellectual. The signs and the planets are rich in symbolism, and the meanings can be very subtle, but it is not possible to go into them in depth here.

Aries — The Ram. A fire sign, ruled by Mars. Loves a challenge and an adventure. Impulsive and headstrong; pioneering, full of initiative.

Taurus — The Bull. An earth sign, ruled by Venus. Patient — as a rule! Loves beauty, art and comfort. Determined, and works hard.

Gemini — The Twins. An air sign, ruled by Mercury. Quick and lively, enjoying all communication and contact with other people. Full of curiosity.

Cancer — The Crab. A water sign, ruled by the moon. Secretive and sensitive. Motherly, and protective of those who are weaker. Moody and imaginative.

Leo — The Lion. A fire sign, ruled by the sun. Likes to be at the centre of attention and activity; creative, and a lover of life. Generous but authoritarian.

Virgo — The Maiden who cuts the corn. An earth sign, ruled by Mercury. Precise, careful in work and very conscientious. Likes to do everything thoroughly, and is interested in matters of health.

Libra — The Scales. An air sign, ruled by Venus. Weighs matters up, and considers carefully before taking action. Likes co-operation and getting on well with other people.

Scorpio — The Scorpion. A water sign, ruled by Mars and Pluto. Passionate and intense. Loyal, ruthless — an "all or nothing" person.

Sagittarius — The Archer. A fire sign, ruled by Jupiter. Loves freedom, space; is very enthusiastic. Humorous, but often a tease.

Capricorn — The Goat. An earth sign, ruled by Saturn. Serious-minded, ambitious, and prudent. Will climb to the top of the mountain even if it takes a lifetime.

Aquarius — The Watercarrier. An air sign, ruled by Saturn and Uranus. Highly individualistic, often unconventional and wilful. A lover of truth; interested in other people and cultures.

Pisces — The Fish. A water sign, ruled by Jupiter and Neptune. Emotional and impressionable. Very changeable according to environment. Artistic, idealistic and "other worldly".

When the chart is drawn, the astrologer will consider each planet, deciding how its position and the sign it is in will influence

▲
8   Aquarius – the sign of the water carrier, from a seventeenth-century book of astrological instruction.

PLANETARY ASPECTS

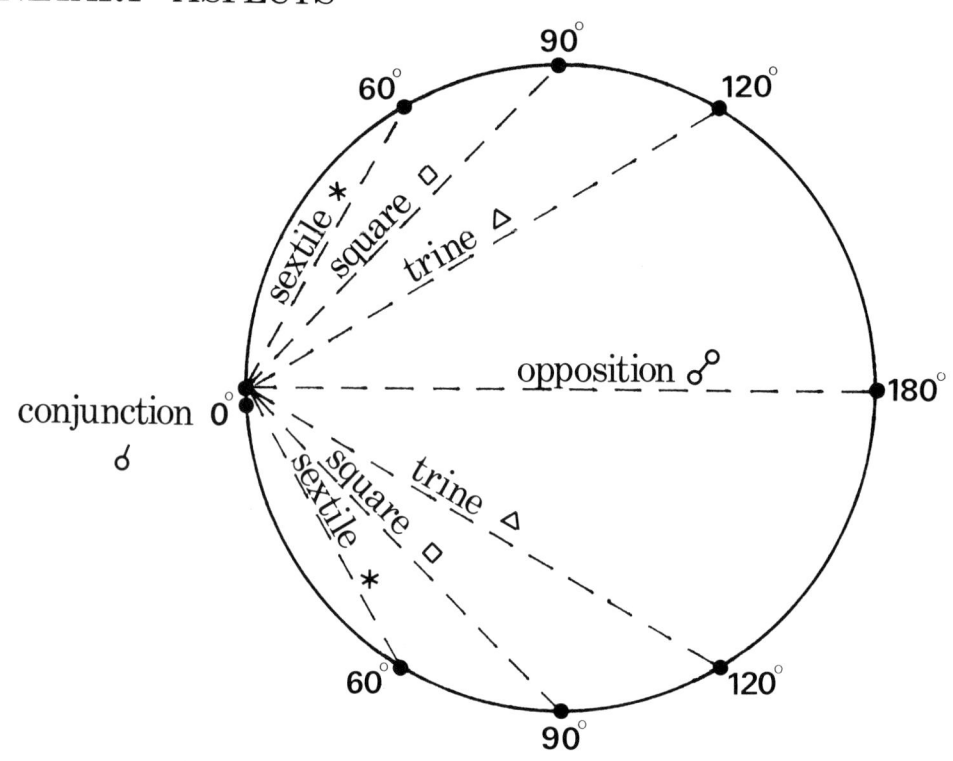

▲
9 This diagram shows the different aspects that can be made between two planets, depending on how many degrees they are apart in the horoscope.

its workings. Mercury, for instance, rules speech. If Mercury is found in Leo, the person concerned will be fond of expressing his opinions and will expect everyone else to take notice of them. He will speak with charm and persuasion, and will often hold the floor. But the astrologer will also look for *aspects* between the planets. Planets influence one another in helpful or unhelpful ways when they are "in aspect" in the chart; two planets are said to be in aspect when they are positioned at a certain angle to one another in the chart; this will be determined by the number of degrees that lie between them in the zodiac. There are five types of major aspect in the horoscope; some produce tension and some an easy flow. If our Mercury in Leo was in square aspect to Neptune, then, as this is a "difficult" aspect, it would bring out some of the disadvantageous side of Neptune, and connect that to the Mercury. Instead of merely enjoying an audience, the person might be tempted to make up tall stories and to boast in order to hold their attention better. But if the Neptune was in "trine", an easy aspect, then the stories would merely be imaginative and fascinating, without any deliberate deception involved.

A full interpretation of a horoscope demands much work from an astrologer. He must try to weigh up all the factors in it, and put them all together in terms of personal characteristics. Astrology can be learnt in the first place from books, but the good astrologer must work with the skill acquired through much experience, in order to practise his art in a creative and helpful way.

2
The Earliest Astrologers

The Babylonians

To find the earliest records of astrology, we must go back at least 4,000 years, to the Middle Eastern kingdom of Babylon. The Babylonians, like most peoples in the world, were fascinated by the sun, moon and stars, and felt their importance in the life of man. But unlike many ancient and tribal peoples, they were not content simply to weave a mythology around them. Instead, they began to observe carefully the movements of the heavenly bodies and to record their findings.

So, at the same time, both astrology and astronomy were born. Nowadays we define astronomy as the science of space, to do with mapping the locations of the stars and planets, and studying their composition. Astrology, the prime concern of this book, is a system of interpreting the positions of the planets, and judging how they indicate conditions and changes in our lives. But it is important to realize that, until the seventeenth century, astronomy and astrology were one subject, and the terms were often used interchangeably. Even the most sceptical people agreed that the stars and planets affected our lives to some degree.

Who were these first astrologers, and how did they work? They were the high priests of the Babylonian culture, which maintained a religion with much emphasis on myths of creation, with deities who revealed themselves in the stars and planets. The priests spent their days and nights in sacred towers, called *ziggurats*. From these, they observed,

10 The remains of the Great Ziggurat of Ur.

calculated, and predicted. At first, their attention was focused upon single omens; the events which interested them most were solar and lunar eclipses. When the light of the sun or the moon was blotted out, it was such an awesome happening that the Babylonians, like many other peoples around the world, were convinced of its relevance to man. The normal pattern of celestial life had been interrupted by something quite extraordinary. But here again, the Babylonians went a stage further; the priests set to work to try to find out if there was a recurring pattern in this disturbing event. They found that there was; and then they were able to predict, to some extent, when the next eclipse was likely to occur. Moreover, the time that the eclipse would take place, and the part of the sky in which it would be visible, had their own symbolic significance, and it was from this that the priests derived their forecasts. For example, in a text by "Irashi-Ilu, the King's servant", we find the following prediction: "On the 14th an eclipse will take place. . . . It is . . . lucky for the King my Lord. Let the King my Lord rest happy."

The first astrological predictions were chiefly concerned with the fate of the ruling king, the state of the weather, and the likelihood of a good harvest. But gradually the priests built up more complex methods that they could use. They learnt to distinguish the planets of our solar system, or "wandering stars", as they were called, since they moved among the stable constellations of the "fixed stars". They saw that the planets did not move at random, but followed a circular path as they passed through the heavens. This they named "The Road of Enlil". (Enlil was the god of the atmosphere.) The planets, called after the Babylonian deities — Marduk, Ishtar, Nergal, and so on — god-like in their attributes, moved through the sacred pathway in the sky.

Then the priests divided this pathway into twelve, and each of the twelve parts was named and given an image — the Ram,

▲
11 This Babylonian boundary stone, c. 1140 BC, shows some of the symbols that came to be associated with the zodiac — the archer, the scorpion, and the bull.

the Bull, the Heavenly Twins, and so on. Thus the zodiac was born. Now these first astrologers could map out, for any moment, the positions of the sun, moon and planets in the zodiac. In short, they had constructed the basis of the horoscope. "Venus in four degrees of the Bull. The place of Venus means: Wherever he goes is favourable. He will have sons and daughters." This is an extract from one of the early horoscopes, preserved on clay tablets, which were the writing materials of the times. The Babylonians left a large collection of predictions and horoscopes, the most famous and extensive of which is called the Enuma Anu Enlil.

Astrology was now established. Its basis was complete by about 400 BC. Experts today are astonished at the mathematical sophistication of these astronomer-priests, who with virtually no apparatus could map and predict the positions of the planets with such accuracy. Yet their conception of the universe was still primitive, by our standards; they saw the earth as a mountain, resting in water, with a domed sky arching above.

The Egyptians

It was left to the enquiring, philosophical mind of the Greeks to investigate the nature of the cosmos further. They were the chief inheritors of the Babylonian astrology. Although Egypt is often considered to be the home of anything occult or mysterious, where astrology is concerned we have very little evidence of the early involvement of the Egyptians. However, they were definitely interested in celestial phenomena and their significance. They invented a calendar that was more effective than that

▲
12 An early instrument, used to aid the calculation of the horoscope (Assyrian period, c. 1000–700 BC).

▲
13 Nut, the goddess of Heaven. She holds the morning sun in her hands. From an Egyptian painting, c. 1000 BC.

of the Babylonians, they gave us a 24-hour day, and 12 months in the year. It is possible that they had a rather different system of astrology which is now lost to us, for they too considered the life of man to be involved with the stars. The heavens were personified by Nut, the sky goddess, brutally separated from her lover, Geb, the earth god, and ever yearning to be reunited with him. The constellations, or the groupings of stars that we see in the sky, were divided by the Egyptians into "decans" or three parts, and each part had its ruling deity.

Much has been written about the Pyramids and temples of Egypt, and plenty of it has been wild speculation. However, it can be proved that many of them were constructed with extreme accuracy to align with astronomical points, such as particular stars, or with the cardinal directions, north, south, east and west. The Great Pyramid of Giza is thought to have been orientated towards the star that marked the north pole at that period. But we do not know what part this played in the symbolism and ritual of the Egyptians.

14 An avenue of ram-headed sphinxes in Egypt. The use of such a symbol (important in astrology as representing Aries, the first sign of the zodiac) suggests that the Egyptians may have had connections with early astrology which we cannot yet prove.
▼

The Greeks

The main thread of the story of astrology, therefore, continues with the Greeks, who seized upon this system of divination eagerly, incorporating it into their culture and developing it. Before the Greeks had had contact with the Babylonian astrologers, or "Chaldeans", as they were known, they had practised mystery religions whose creed was that a man's soul journeyed through the planetary regions on its voyage to heaven. A system such as astrology, which could show how the planets related to man here on earth in his daily life, would be a very satisfying development of this theme.

Many theories of cosmology, that is, of how the world was constructed, were proposed by the Greeks. The earlier view was that the universe was composed of eight concentric spheres, seven of which were ruled by the planets.

◀15 The Great Pyramid, seen towering behind the inscrutable gaze of the famous Sphinx.

This theme was developed by the great philosopher, Plato (thought to have lived 428—348 BC). He saw the universe as a spherical, harmonious whole, united like a living body. In such a universe all is related, and it is thus natural that the planets should be involved in our lives and we in theirs. Plato, Aristotle, and the Stoic philosophers produced very deep and complex arguments to show the interrelation of man and the heavens. The theory of astrology fitted very well into the philosophy of a harmonious and integrated world.

Using this philosophy as their basis, the Greeks began to try to explain the workings of stars, space, and of the material world around them. They were inspired by the idea of a universe constructed according to laws and principles; they were not content to stay with the old creation myths, but desired to observe afresh, and to use reason in their new scientific formulations. Such enthusiasm brought about important discoveries. Eratosthenes was the first man to devise a method for measuring the circumference of the earth. Hipparchus compiled a catalogue of the fixed stars, and made a bold attempt to measure the distance between the moon and the earth. Aristarchus made an even more remarkable discovery — although his ideas were largely rejected for another 1800 years or so. In about 300 BC he proposed that the sun did not move around the earth, but the earth around the sun. The theory was too revolutionary for the day — scarcely anyone was ready to consider that they were not at the centre of the universe! Other cosmological theories were expounded, and much clever and ingenious deduction went into them.

In about 280 BC, the first school of Greek astrology was established on the island of Cos. Whereas the Babylonians had chiefly

16 A Victorian artist's impression of the observatory of Hipparchus, the ancient astronomer.
▼

interested themselves in casting horoscopes for kings and nobles, the Greeks took astrology into every class of society, and busied themselves with studying how the patterns of people's lives were reflected in their horoscopes. Some of their case-books survive, and make fascinating reading. One of the most famous astrologers of the period whose work we have is Vettius Valens, who lived in the second century AD. He, like the other astrologers of the period, was interested in seeing how the fortunes of a man evolve, how he might rise to certain heights on the "Wheel of Fortune" and then fall again. In one of his case-books he writes:

Sun and Jupiter in Capricorn, Moon and Saturn in Leo, Mars in Pisces. . . . He was a dancer, and in his 25th year was put in confinement in the course of a public riot, but he was defended before the governor and released . . . and became more esteemed. The nativity was precarious as regards loss of reputation . . . and danger of life. But Venus being found in the Ascendant . . . and Jupiter with the Sun, it had the best imaginable outcome.

One of the greatest astrologers of all time was a Greek, born in Alexandria — Ptolemy. We know that he lived and worked around AD 100, but have very few details of his personal life. He is famous in astrological history for his great work, the *Tetrabiblos* ("Four Books") which sets out astrological practice with lucidity and thoroughness. He clarified what was by then a much expanded and confused system of astrology, for the enthusiasm with which astrology had been hailed by the Greeks was responsible for many new techniques and differences in interpretation. Ptolemy put it all together, and formulated the astrological system with such persuasion and insight that his works became the standard reference books for astrologers for centuries, and, indeed, are still in use today.

The Romans

If the Greeks took astrology into the home of the common man, the Romans took it out onto the streets. The Roman diviners had previously used such methods of fortune-telling as examining the entrails of slaughtered animals, or observing the flight of birds. Astrology was introduced to Rome by the Greeks and Chaldeans, many of whom were brought in as captives or slaves. Although astrology appeared in the Roman Empire as early as the third century BC, its great flowering came after the beginning of the Christian era. The general reaction to it was somewhat suspicious at first, but the Roman diviners soon picked up the art and turned it into a cash business! Some made a speciality of trying to predict the winners of chariot races. Others were willing to cast your horoscope at a street corner, and what they did not know they would make up. Many of these must have been charlatans; astrology practised properly was still an occupation for learned men, as the calculations involved were considerable, and the interpretation then, as now, was a very complex matter needing much study of the techniques and symbolism.

Astrology still had a place at a more serious level. One of the most famous Roman astrologers was Marcus Manilius, who lived in the first century AD. He wrote a splendid book in poetry about the nature of astrology. It is not a complete text book, but it sparkles with life and insight. His description of the individual sun signs is as vivid and relevant today as it was nearly 2,000 years ago.

From the Twins [Gemini] come less laborious callings and a more agreeable way of life . . . those so endowed find even work a pleasure. They would banish the arms of war, the trumpet's call and the gloom of old age: theirs is a life of ease and unfading youth spent in the arms of love. They also discover paths to the

17 The Romans adopted astrology with enthusiasm. The signs of the zodiac were used to decorate an amulet of the period, of which this is an engraving.

skies, complete a survey of the heavens with numbers and measurements, and outstrip the flight of the stars.

Even today, astronomy is reckoned to be an appropriate study for Geminians!

The emperors of Rome saw another use for astrology — and they feared yet desired this knowledge. If astrology could predict the future, might it forecast their rise to power? But worse, might it show their eventual downfall? Such information was dangerous, and succeeding emperors oscillated between courting the favour of astrologers, and being delighted with their prophecies (as Augustus was when the astrologer Theagenes forecast that he would become ruler of the land), and expressing hostility (as did Tiberius who ordered various people to be put to death for casting horoscopes).

Politicians became more and more suspicious of astrology, and the public became disenchanted with the fraudulent practice of it which they encountered. Fewer astrologers were concerned with the fundamental spiritual and cosmological issues that had fascinated the Greeks; many were treating astrology as a cash commodity, and producing their predictions with over-confidence. The Roman Empire declined, and so did astrology, and it was only the Arabs who kept it alive for hundreds of years.

3
Magic and Medicine — Astrology in Medieval England

Until the great revival of learning in Europe in the twelfth century, the English were scarcely acquainted with astrology. But there had already been a tradition of interest in the power of the planets, and in charting the movements of the heavenly bodies. Around 2,000 BC the native peoples constructed hundreds of impressive stone circles and avenues in Britain. The most famous of these is Stonehenge. For centuries after this culture died out, no one knew what the monuments had been built for, and many superstitions and legends grew up around them. Some said that the fairies dwelt in them, and that beautiful music issued forth which would fatally enchant any mortal. Others had heard tales of fabulous treasure buried there. It is only in the twentieth century that painstaking research shows up a different purpose for these carefully built circles. It now appears that they were constructed to act as astronomical signposts, pointers indicating timings and celestial locations of such events as eclipses and solstices.

Much later, after the Roman occupation of Britain, the people continued their interest in the heavens by worshipping the sun and moon. We know this, because a law was passed in the time of King Canute in the eleventh century, forbidding them to do so! Such a practice would be blasphemous in the now Christian country. In the early medieval period, the English had their own, rather crude kind of astrology where various predictions were made, based on the cycle of the moon. If you were born on the first day of the moon you were expected to be long-lived and wealthy — but, alas! if on the 23rd night, you would be a thief and a seamp!

It is the Arabs who were responsible for keeping the mainstream of astrology alive after the decline of the Roman Empire. In

18 Standing stones at Callernish, in the Hebrides; an example of an ancient stone complex in which astronomical alignments have been discovered.

the eighth century AD a school of astrology was founded in Baghdad. One of its most famous pupils was Albumazar, who wrote an astrological textbook which became very popular in Europe later. He, like all the Arabian astrologers, was interested in *horary* astrology and *electional* astrology. Horary is a branch of astrology which is the answering of questions from a given moment in time. If, for instance, a man wanted to know whether his son would come home safely from the war, he would ask the astrologer, who would draw up a horoscope for the time the question was asked, and by applying various rules and skills of interpretation, could give the man an answer. Horary astrology became well-established in England later, as we shall see. Electional astrology is the art of choosing a good moment to start a particular project, whether it be a marriage, a coronation, or the founding of a university. The astrologer endeavours to calculate when the most suitable and auspicious planetary influences will occur, and draws up a complete horoscope for the projected time. The Arabs investigated these branches of astrology, and wrote many instructions for carrying them out, which their European successors made use of gratefully.

One of the first English astrologers was Adelard of Bath who lived in the twelfth century. He was a traveller, and visited countries as far away as Syria. He translated some of the Arabic astrological texts which had not been available before. He left us some writing of his own upon astrology, including this glowing description of the art:

She appears, surrounded by shining splendour.... In her right hand she holds a quadrant, in her left hand an astrolabe.... If a man acquire this science of astronomy, he will obtain knowledge, not only of the present condition of the world, but of the past and future as well.

19 Albumazar, the famous Arabian astrologer. The picture is from an early sixteenth-century edition of his major work on astronomy and astrology, translated from Arabic into Latin for the use of European scholars.

(Remember that the terms astrology and astronomy were used interchangeably.)

On the whole, the Italians and the French were quicker to pick up the study of astrology than the English, beginning their enquiries into the ancient tradition in the eleventh and twelfth centuries. The school at Chartres was one of the most advanced in learning, and students there read not only Arabic texts, but classical Greek and Latin ones too. Aristotle's and Plato's works were now available, and caused much excitement among scholars. Those interested in astronomy and astrology could relate the philosophy and cosmology of the ancients to their study.

The Church had mixed feelings about the revival of interest in astrology. St Augustine (AD 354-430) had roundly condemned it, and called astrological prediction the work of the devil, even though he, like most people of the time, accepted that the stars and planets do relate to human life in some way.

20 The appearance of a comet usually caused alarm and apprehension. It was seen as a portent, often of harm that would befall a reigning monarch. Halley's comet appeared in 1066, and here, the Bayeux tapestry, woven in the twelfth century, records the sighting. 1066, of course, was the year that King Harold of England was killed when the Normans invaded.

In the medieval period, Thomas Aquinas, a wise theologian, sought to argue that the use of astrology was respectable, and acceptable to the Christian religion, provided that it was kept within certain limits. He, and other moderate churchmen of the day, said that our horoscopes affect us mainly through our bodies, shaping us, and implanting in us various personality traits. But that does not mean that man need give in to all these inclinations; man has free will and can rise above them if they are undesirable.

Astrology rapidly grew in popularity, and became so esteemed that it was studied in universities. However, many astrologers must have taken it as a warning not to go too far in their pronouncements when, in 1327, the professor of astrology at the University of Bologna was put to death. His judges said that his astrology contained too much magic, and he had made the great theological mistake of saying that the birth and life of Christ were subject to a horoscope. Since Christ was considered divine, it was thought heretical to say that the planets should have any influence over him. Others would argue, however, that his birth had after all been foretold by astrologers — the Three Magi, who had seen "a star in the east".

For a time, in England, many of the astrologers came from foreign countries. They were much in demand at the royal court, and it is said that they were kept hard at work drawing up horoscopes to try to predict the outcome of the wars between England and France, which lasted from 1337-1453. National predictions were treated seriously. In 1186 most European astrologers had forecast catastrophe, when a conjunction of planets was expected in Libra. Terrific winds and devastating earthquakes were among their prophecies for a large part of the earth's surface! The English astrologers were not left behind in this race to predict disaster, and thought that England would be particularly vulnerable. Many people took to caves and underground hiding places to avoid the expected trouble. However, nothing greatly unusual is recorded as having happened! Comets and eclipses were still treated as unpleasant omens too.

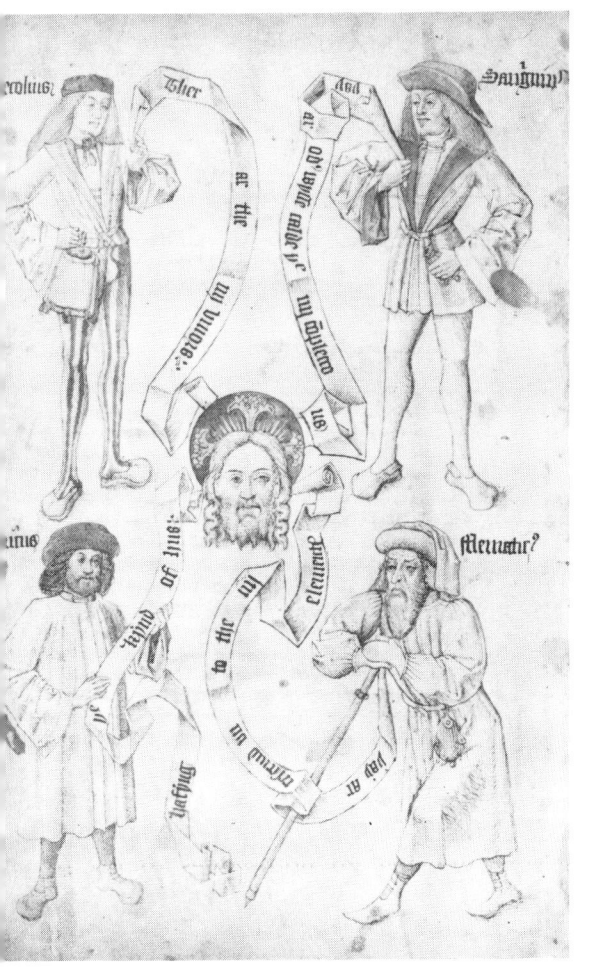

Astrology in Medicine

One of the growing uses of astrology was in medicine. Many doctors took their learning from Galen, a Roman astrologer-physician of the second century AD. Galen had refined and developed the Greek theory that the world, and man himself, was composed of four elements: earth, air, fire and water. In man, these elements were known as the four "humours" or "temperaments", and they were called melancholic, sanguine, choleric and phlegmatic, respectively. They related to the zodiac too, where every sign is ruled by one of the elements. Diseases were thought to be caused by an imbalance of a particular humour. Additionally, each part of the body, in astrological tradition, is said to be ruled by a sign of the zodiac. A person's horoscope would give useful information as to which areas of his body were particularly weak or likely to succumb to disease, and the doctor could use this as an aid to diagnosis and treatment. In his *Prologue* to *The Canterbury Tales*, the poet Chaucer describes a party of pilgrims setting off to visit Canterbury. He gives us a lively picture of a typical doctor of the day:

> *With us ther was a DOCTOUR of PHISYK,*
> *In al this world ne was ther noon him lyk*
> *To speke of phisik and of surgerye;*
> *For he was grounded in astronomye.*
> *He kepte his pacient a ful greet del*
> *In houres, by his magik naturel.*
> *Wel coude he fortunen the ascendent*
> *Of his images for his pacient.*
> *He knew the cause of everich maladye*
> *Were it of hoot or cold, or moist or drye,*
> *And where engendred, and of what humour;*
> *He was a verrey parfit practisour.*

◀ 21 The Four Humours and the types of men they represented. From top right clockwise: sanguine, phlegmatic, choleric and melancholic.

23

The PARTS of Mans Body as it is governed distinctly by the Twelve Signes.

♈ Head and Face.

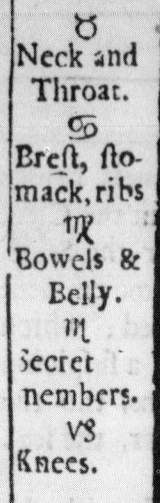

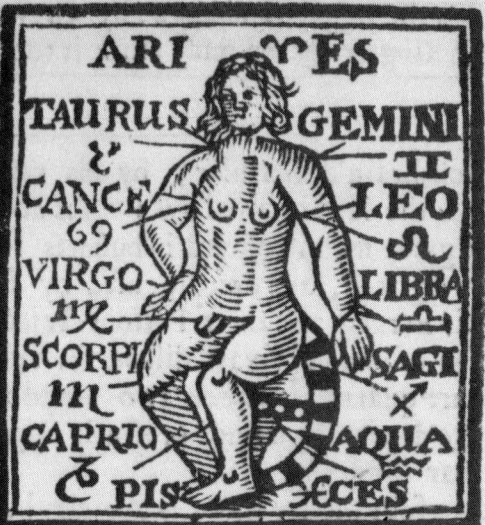

♉ Neck and Throat.
♋ Brest, stomack, ribs
♍ Bowels & Belly.
♏ Secret members.
♑ Knees.

♊ Arms and shoulder.
♌ Heart and back.
♎ Reins and loyns.
♐ Thighs.
♒ Legs.

♓ The Feet.

The working Head is govern'd by the *Ram*.
And Head-strong *Taurus* rules the Neck of Man.
The Twins gives to the Arms and Shoulders Laws.
And on the Breast the Crab-fish claps his Claws.
The *Lyon* rules the back; and let me tell ye,
The modest Maid carefully guides the Belly.
The serious Reins to *Libra* given were.
The restless Secrets to the *Scorpion's* care.
The Thighs do to the Horseman Homage shew.
And *Capricornus* claims the Knees as due.
The Legs they are the Water-bearers Fee.
Pisces supports the Feet, you plainly see.

Sapiens dominabitur Astris.

◀ 22   A delightful poetical version of the rulership of the zodiac signs over parts of the body. From *Partridge's Almanack*, 1683.

Medicine could be supplemented by magical talismans. A talisman was an appropriate image for the planet whose vital forces were sought — a lion, for instance, for the sun — and it would be made carefully in the right materials and at the proper planetary hour.

It is noted that every true act must be done under his planet. And it is better if it be done in the proper day of the planet, and in his own proper hour.
(From *The Book of Secrets of Albertus Magnus*)

Each hour of each day was thought to be ruled by a particular planet. The first hour after sunrise was ruled by the planet of the day — for example, Saturn for Saturday — and the other hours were divided up among the following planets. The hours were of different lengths, depending on the length of daylight. Planetary hours were also used in gathering herbs for the medicines.

Each herb was ruled by a planet. This was part of a great cosmological structuring that was revered in medieval and Elizabethan times. The universe was thought of as made in descending levels of creation. The planets were high up on the scale, below only the angels and God himself. Below the planets came different categories of life on earth — animals, plants, minerals, etc, and all could be related back to the powerful planets. Thus each plant, animal, bird and precious stone was ruled by a particular planet, sharing in its qualities and strengths. To use the power of Mars, for instance, perhaps to heal a wound or to protect oneself in battle, one would prepare a medicine of herbs ascribed to Mars, or make a talisman in the image of Mars. The planets were thought of as pure, unchanging, and holy in their closeness to the Immortal. Only in the "sub-lunary" sphere, the realm below the moon, containing life on earth, were matters thought to be subject to change and decay.

23   Even different parts of the face were considered to be ruled by different signs and planets. This particular picture would have been used for reference by astrologers and certain medical practitioners of the seventeenth century. The medieval physicians would have used a very similar diagram.
▼

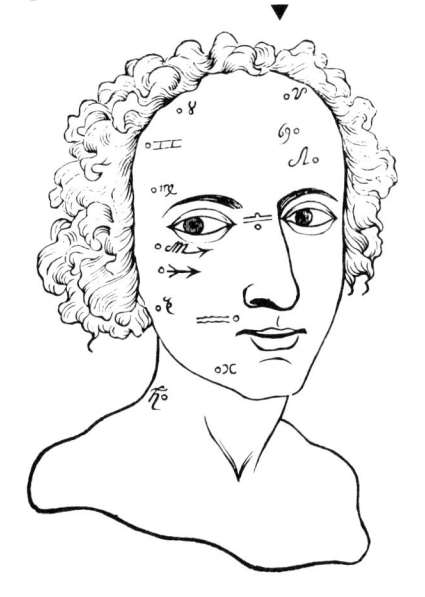

25

24 An example of correspondences: — associations between different birds and planets are shown in this fourteenth-century English manuscript. The peacock appears against the sun, the raven against Saturn.

25 A beautiful illustration from a manuscript of *The Complaint of Mars and Venus*.

Medieval Horoscopes

On a more mundane level, the English astrologers of the late medieval period drew up charts for their clients, and made pronouncements with great confidence. To modern eyes, many of their readings seem too black-and-white in quality. Saturn and Mars were known as the "malefics", and were said to cause woe and destruction in whatever part of life they touched upon in the natal chart. Venus and Jupiter, on the other hand, were called "benefics", and brought good fortune and pleasant times where they reigned. Not all astrologers were simplistic in approach, though. Roger Bacon, an English friar, famous for his early and revolutionary approach to science, was an accomplished astrologer and a deep thinker. He condemned the astrologers who were mere shallow conjurors, defiling their art by "very silly characters, and very foolish incantations, and irrational speeches".

By the time Chaucer was writing in the fourteenth century, astrology was popular enough to be woven into his poems and tales. He wrote a complete poem on *The Complaint of Mars and Venus*, treating the planets as a pair of lovers, who bewailed their fate in being parted when the different speed of their orbits separated them! In *The Canterbury Tales* the Wife of Bath excuses her amorous nature thus:

For certes, I am al Venerien
In felinge, and myn herte is Marcien.
Venus me yaf my lust, my likerousnesse,
And Mars yaf me my sturdy hardinesse.
Myn ascendent was Taur, and Mars therinne.

And, indeed, astrologers today would be inclined to give much the same interpretation to a lady with Mars in Taurus on the ascendant of the horoscope!

Chaucer also wrote, for his "little son Lewis", a treatise on the astrolabe. The astrolabe was the most common instrument in use to determine the degree of the zodiac rising, and other factors of the horoscope. It was a complex arrangement of dials and inscriptions, and was set to a particular latitude.

Although astrology, as we see from Chaucer's many casual references to it, was part of the common knowledge of the English people by the close of the medieval period, yet to construct and interpret a horoscope was still the province of a man of learning. Books were hand-written and expensive, and reading and calculating were still the work of monks and scholars.

26 An astrolabe from the seventeenth century, a later period.
▼

4
Astrology in England, 1450-1700 — Food for Philosophers, Priests and Poets

The period 1450-1700 was one of great change and development in the arts and sciences throughout Europe. Although writers and thinkers still paid tribute to the doctrines of the Church, and to the authority of classical writers, they were no longer firmly bound by these dictates. There was a spirit of freedom and progress which encouraged men to look afresh at all the matters they had previously taken for granted. Astrology itself was reappraised, questioned and argued over. This was the time when astrology reached the peak of its popularity and influence in England, and it is found in nearly every level of contemporary culture, from common expressions and jokes to the most learned philosophical discussions. Yet it was during this period that the seeds were sown for a new world picture that eventually undermined the public confidence in astrology.

From 1450 to 1700, astrology first blossomed and then withered away. It blossomed because of the new impetus of thought and enquiry that arose early in the period, and it withered, ultimately, because of the startling new discoveries in the field of astronomy.

Although people in the middle ages argued over the minor details of how the universe was arranged, they were still happy with the idea that the planets revolved in their spheres around a central earth. But in the sixteenth century Nicholas Copernicus showed that it was possible to account for the movements of the planets by setting the sun at the centre, and giving the earth only a minor role as another mere planet revolving around it. This concept was so offensive to those who heard it that it was not taken seriously till nearly a hundred years later.

While the public took their time to digest this startling suggestion, other discoveries were following thick and fast. Tycho Brahe, a Danish astronomer (1564-1601), was able to prove that a comet which appeared in 1577 must lie beyond the sphere of the moon. If something new had appeared in the "unchanging" world beyond the moon, then the realm of the stars and planets was subject to changes just as we were on earth. At the beginning of the seventeenth century the telescope was invented, and excited professionals and amateurs alike saw that the moon was pitted with craters, and that Jupiter had moons of its own. Copernicus had proposed a sun-centred universe, but now the Italian Giordano Bruno (1548-1600) said that our solar system was one of an infinite number, and that the far-away stars were really suns like our own, with their own planetary systems — perhaps even inhabited!

Later, the German, Johannes Kepler (1571-1630) was able to show conclusively that the planets revolve in elliptical orbits around the sun — and the age of celestial

PTOLOMAIC SYSTEM   COPERNICAN SYSTEM

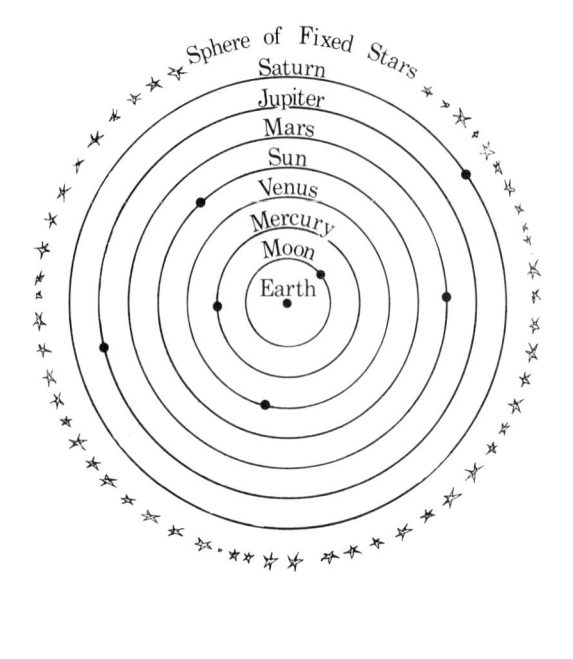

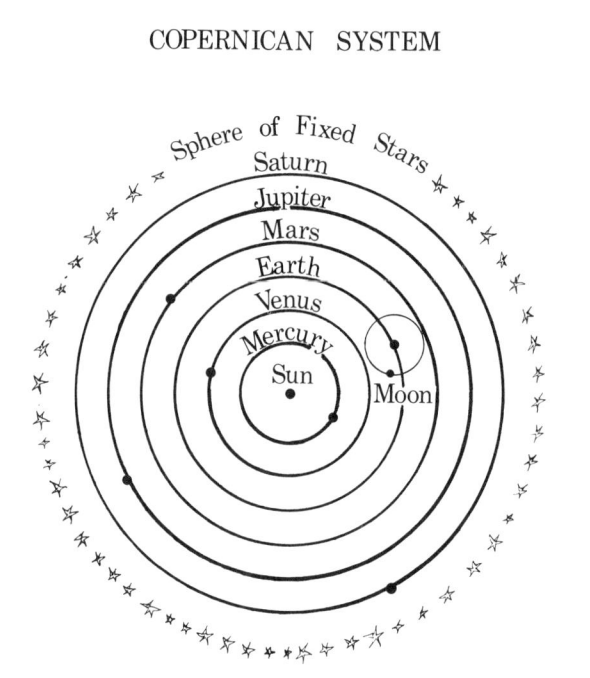

▲
27 In the Ptolomaic view of the world, all planets revolved around the earth. Ptolemy, in the second century AD, accounted for the irregular motion of the planets by a complicated system of "epicycles", or extra little orbits made by the planets as they revolved in their spheres. The Ptolomaic view held sway throughout medieval times, until the general acceptance of Copernican cosmology in the sixteenth and seventeenth centuries.

▲
28 Copernicus, who was born in Poland and lived from 1473–1543, saw that the earth was a planet and went round the sun. However, he thought that the sun itself was the centre of the Universe.

spheres was no more. All these scientific developments must have helped to fuel the debate about the truth of astrology. The philosophers of the Italian Renaissance had sparked off arguments for and against astrology, and these were carried on vigorously on English soil. Unlike the Italians, who published in Latin, the English tended to write in their own language, and with the introduction of the printing press, this meant that books and pamphlets became available to a wide audience.

Priests and men of religion were not always happy about the implications of astrology, especially when, in its extreme forms, it denied that man had any choice in his actions. Could it really be, as Webster, the early seventeenth-century dramatist, said: "We are merely the stars' tennis balls, struck and banded which way please them"? From the moderate astrologers came the reply that to be forewarned is to be forearmed, and that man can master his stars, rather than let them conquer him. William Fulke, one of the first Englishmen to publish an attack on astrology (in 1560), did not agree. Although he accepted some of the unlikely and superstitious elements of the tradition, such as the belief that a bay tree was immune to lightning because it was ruled by Jupiter, he poured scorn on the practice of horoscope-making:

O blockhead, that thou must have thy nativity cast, how dost thou determine to lead thy life, like a brute beast, that thou will suffer all things to work upon thee.

John Chamber, another enemy of astrology, asked sarcastically in his *Treatise against Judicial Astrology*, 1601, why astrologers did not draw up horoscopes for nests of eggs, since they believed the planets to affect the destiny of everything on earth. Sir Christopher Heydon, in a lengthy and pedantic reply, retorted that, in his observation, most people who attacked astrology were those who had tried to practise it in the past. But, not being clever enough to master its subtleties, they turned against it in spite!

The scholars might argue its merits, but astrology was still an intrinsic part of daily life in England. Astrologers were involved in politics and in the lives of kings and queens. Henry VIII, famous for his many wives, was partial to discussions on astrology and astronomy, and was treated in illness

29   Could man go beyond the stars, and find Eternity the other side, as this Swiss drawing of about 1500 suggests? Until the astronomical discoveries of the sixteenth and seventeenth centuries, it was thought possible.
▼

▲
30 There was tremendous interest in astronomy during the sixteenth and seventeenth centuries. In this seventeenth-century drawing a man is seen taking a measurement of the sun's angle from on board ship. There was a desperate need for better astronomical instruments for sea navigation.

by physicians who used astrological theory in their cures. The most famous astrologer at court was undoubtedly John Dee (1527-1608), who served Queen Elizabeth I. He was a remarkable man, a skilled astrologer, but also interested in magic, religion, archaeology and science. He was equally at home using a pendulum to divine missing objects (a practice called dowsing nowadays) as he was constructing precision instruments for sea navigation, and he moved in many circles of learned men, at home and abroad.

Elizabeth took him into her confidence from very early on. As a girl, she was in semi-captivity while her sister, Mary Tudor, was on the throne, and Dee managed to keep in contact with her to instruct her in astrology and any sciences that she took an interest in. When her fortunes changed, and she was to become Queen, she asked Dee to choose, astrologically, a suitable Coronation Day for her. The year was 1558; he chose the day of Sunday 15 January. The Coronation was a huge success, although foreign ambassadors criticized the familiar way in which the Queen moved among her delighted subjects. Later, when she considered marriage, she

31 A sixteenth-century astronomer in his study. He probably has no interest in astrology. For him, astronomy has become a separate profession.

again asked Dee to look at the planetary indications. He saw marriage as inappropriate for her, and it seems that she was relieved. Her sun sign, incidentally, was Virgo, symbolized by the Virgin maiden, a striking image for the Queen who rejected all suitors for her hand. She remained in contact with Dee throughout her life, and it is believed that he worked as a spy for her at certain times.

In 1603 Elizabeth died. James, her successor, is famous for his vehement attacks upon witchcraft, and anything that had a hint of magic about it. Although Dee himself was not prosecuted, he fell from favour, and ended his life in great poverty. In certain high quarters it was muttered that astrologers were no better than witches, and should be treated as such.

Astrology escaped open persecution, however, and if we look at the literature of the whole period, we find that it is studded with references to horoscopes, planets, and signs of the zodiac. Astrological terms were common figures of speech: "Oh my stars!" was a favourite expression, as was "blessed stars", or "ill planets", depending on whether the speaker's luck was in or out at the time! Many poets and playwrights embroidered their work with astrological imagery, and

▲
32 A fifteenth-century illustration of Dante's *Inferno*. Dante (1265–1321) wrote *The Divine Comedy*, which relates a journey through hell, purgatory and heaven. In hell (the *Inferno*) fortune-tellers are seen, with their gaze fixed eternally backwards — a punishment for trying to look ahead when they were alive on earth!

the poet, George Chapman (1559–1634) even used it as the basis for a complete work, called *The Amorous Zodiac*.

Shakespeare's references to astrology in his plays have fascinated many generations. He drew on his knowledge of it to add to his writing at all levels, from the deepest discussions of life's meaning, to ready jokes that would have raised an instant laugh from the audience of the day. Today's playgoer would need to brush up on his astrological knowledge to be amused! In *Twelfth Night* that foolish pair, Sir Andrew Aguecheek and Sir Toby Belch, are discussing whether to hold some revels:

Sir Toby: — *What shall we do else? were we not born under Taurus?*
Sir Andrew: — *Taurus! that's sides and heart.*
Sir Toby: — *No sir, it is legs and thighs. Let me see thee caper. Ha! higher; ha ha! excellent!*

They have been referring to the parts of the body ruled by the zodiac signs; but, of course, they have got it wrong! Taurus rules the throat.

In *All's Well that Ends Well* Shakespeare uses astrological imagery to switch the mood from joking to seriousness. Helena at first laughs with the puffed-up soldier, Parolles:

Helena: — *The wars have kept you so much under that you must needs be born under Mars.*
Parolles: — *When he was predominant.*
Helena: — *When he was retrograde, I think rather.*
Parolles: — *Why think you so?*
Helena: — *You go so much backwards when you fight.*

But a few moments later, left to herself, she muses:

*Our remedies oft in ourselves do lie
Which we ascribe to heaven: the fated sky
Gives us free scope; only doth backward pull
Our slow designs when we are dull.*

33 A contemporary woodcut of Jupiter and Mars. ▶

in feriozes significet accidētia q̄ fiūt in breuibus tēporibus cū significationibus eorū
in tēporibus longis apparent successiue ꝯtinuatio eoꝝ diuersificeꞇ in situ in oibus
tēporibus ꞇ pparent signationes eoꝝ in illis oibus tēporibus frequenter ꞇ successiue
ꞇ reuolubiliter. ℂHinc littera suspensiua est interpositionib⁹. Itē cū magis necesse
vt veniā cū signationibus eoꝝ ſm̄ accidentia in hora reuolutionuꝫ tēpoꝝ q̄ predixi
mus ex pte descensus quorundā apud quosdā sup oēs ptes figurarum vt si vnum
adiuuantiuꝫ sup declarationē impressionuꝫ supioꝝ induiduoꝝ in accidētibus infe
rioribus ſm̄ q̄ pmisimus. Rememoremus itaq̄ in hoc tractatu significationē pla
netarum ꞇ cōmixtionem quorundā adinuiceꝫ in signationibus suis adiutorio dei.

ℂDicamus ergo q̄m cōiunctio
duoꝝ supioꝝ scꝫ saturni ꞇ iouis
planetarum fecit aliq̄d ex rebus
necessario in pmutatiōib⁹ secta
ruꝫ ꞇ vitiuꝫ ꞇ pmutationibus le
guꝫ ꞇ instructionibus ꞇ in aduē
tu ingentiuꝫ reꝫ ꞇ in pmutatiōe
imperij ꞇ in morte reguꝫ ꞇ in ad
uentu ppherarum ꞇ pphetiꝫādi
ꞇ miraculoꝝ in sectis ꞇ vicibus
regnoꝝ sicut pmisimus fuit pp
cōmixtionē reliquoꝝ planetaruꝫ
ꞇ cōtinuationē eoꝝ adinuiceꝫ in
reliquis figuris cuꝫ multis signi
ficationibus sup res q̄ apparent
in aliquo annoꝝ totaliuꝫ sup sectas ꞇ vices annoꝝ significatiū ex actionib⁹ reguꝫ ꞇ
plebis; oēs vero ꝯiunctiōes iouis cuꝫ saturno ꞇ cū planetis ex reliq̄s figuris tracta
bimus in hac ora. ℂDicamus itaq̄ q̄ cū ꝯtinuaꞇ iupiter cum saturno ex ✱ vel △
aspectu sigt illud apparētiā ornātiuꝫ ꞇ reguꝫ ꞇ nobiliuꝫ ꞇ pphetie ꞇ pphetāḏi ꞇ secre
toꝝ. Et cuꝫ fuerit illud ex quadratura ꞇ fuerit ex quarto signaꞇ tegumentū ornantiū
ꞇ querentiuꝫ regnū ꞇ exaltationē multaꝝ reꝫ de rebus secte ꞇ fidei. Et si fuerit ex.7.

signat multitudinē rixaruꝫ inter
ciues impij ꞇ gētes ꞇ multitudi
nē terribiliuꝫ rerūꝫ ꞇ si fuerit illd
ex. 10. sigt multitudinē rixaꝝ iter
gētes ꞇ tetradas ꞇ iudices.

ℂPostq̄ aūt pmisim⁹ in ora. 8.
tractatus scdi signationes ꝯiun
ctiōis ♂ ꞇ ♄ i oib⁹ signis: ꞇ fue
rit de pprietate ei⁹ vehemētia ad
uēt⁹ variolaꝝ ꞇ vlceꝝ ꞇ plagaꝝ ꞇ
fraudis ꞇ deceptiōis ꞇ iactatiōis
ꞇ renouationis regni hoieꝫ in ter
ra illius signi in quo cōiungunꞇ
cum eo q̄ appropriauim⁹ de eo
in oibus signis singulariter. Re

· IVPITER ·

34   Astrology in art reached great heights. Here is a fine manuscript illustration of Jupiter, by an Italian artist. Directly below Jupiter are seen the emblems for Pisces and Sagittarius, the signs which Jupiter rules. At the bottom of the picture we see images of trading and harvest, symbolic of the rich plenty attributed to Jupiter.

In other fields, especially medicine, astrology was still important. In 1437, in Paris, there had been a controversy as to which were the most suitable days for blood-letting, a remedy much in favour at the time. The arbitrators recommended that every physician should possess an astrolabe, so that he could work out the ascending sign and compare it to the sign of the moon, to see if the conditions were favourable. The appearance of syphilis in Europe was thought to be due to a conjunction of four planets in Scorpio, in 1484. Scorpio, ruling the private parts of the body, would have a natural association with a sexual disease. And the very name "influenza", popularly shortened to "flu" today, means "star influence". A comet which shone in 1529 was related, said one astrologer, to the plague of sweating-sickness which broke out in England that year.

Astrology was not yet a dying relic in the sciences. It was practised by Paracelsus, the great Swiss doctor, who profoundly influenced the course of medicine in the following centuries. He attacked the physicians of the time who learnt medicine without ever seeing a live patient, and who took as gospel all the ancient, outworn teachings handed down to them. Paracelsus treated the rich and the poor alike, and he travelled to find the wise men, the gipsies and peasant healers of other countries and to learn from them. He saw his work as a spiritual path, and the doctor as a servant and messenger of God, whose duty was to be open to new discoveries. Paracelsus used astrology, and took his patients' horoscopes and the planetary rulerships of minerals and plants into account in treatment. But he did not subscribe to a blind, fatalistic faith in astrology:

The stars are subject to the philosopher, they must follow him and not he them. Only the man who is still animal is governed, mastered, compelled and driven by the stars.

Astrology was part of the pathway to immortality studied by such close-knit occult groups of the seventeenth century as the Rosicrucians. Robert Fludd (1574-1637), one of their most famous members, published books and diagrams which present a cosmic scheme of man and the universe, in which the planets represent higher forces in the world of man. In this tradition, and in the related alchemical system, where men sought to turn base metal into gold (an analogy for the transformation of the

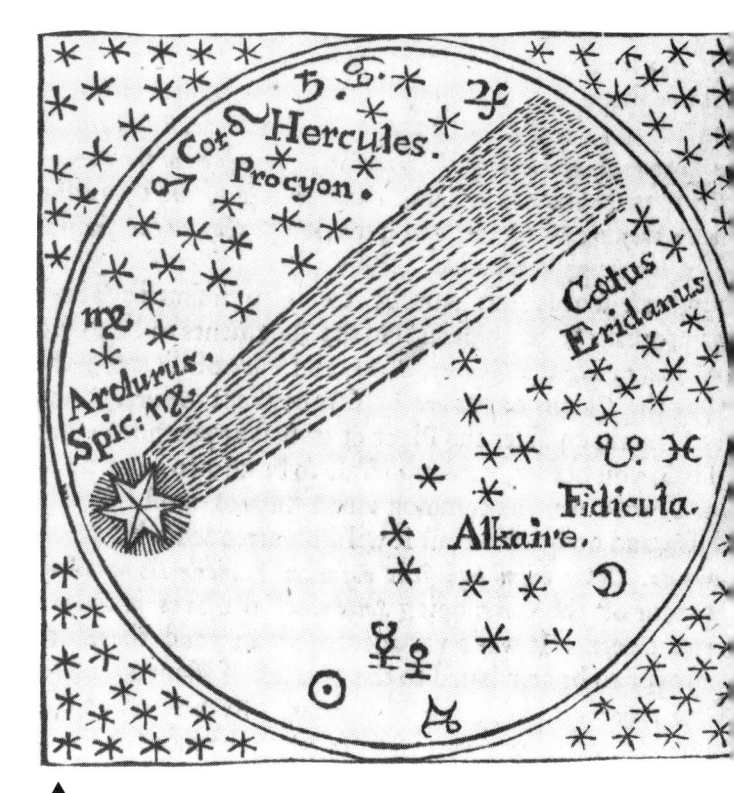

35   Comets were still regarded with awe, and their horoscopes drawn up and interpreted. This is from an almanack of 1683.

36 Heinrich Cornelius Agrippa (1486–1535) was a man of many talents: he worked as a physician, theologian, university lecturer and court secretary. He is remembered chiefly for his magical writings which influenced many people of the period, particularly those who were searching for a hidden meaning in the world around them. Here is one of his diagrams representing the planets in relation to the human body.
▼

soul), astrology took on a very specialized form. Mercury, for instance, has a significance that makes it the great key to the whole alchemical process, and it is impossible to read alchemical or Rosicrucian texts in the light of ordinary astrological knowledge.

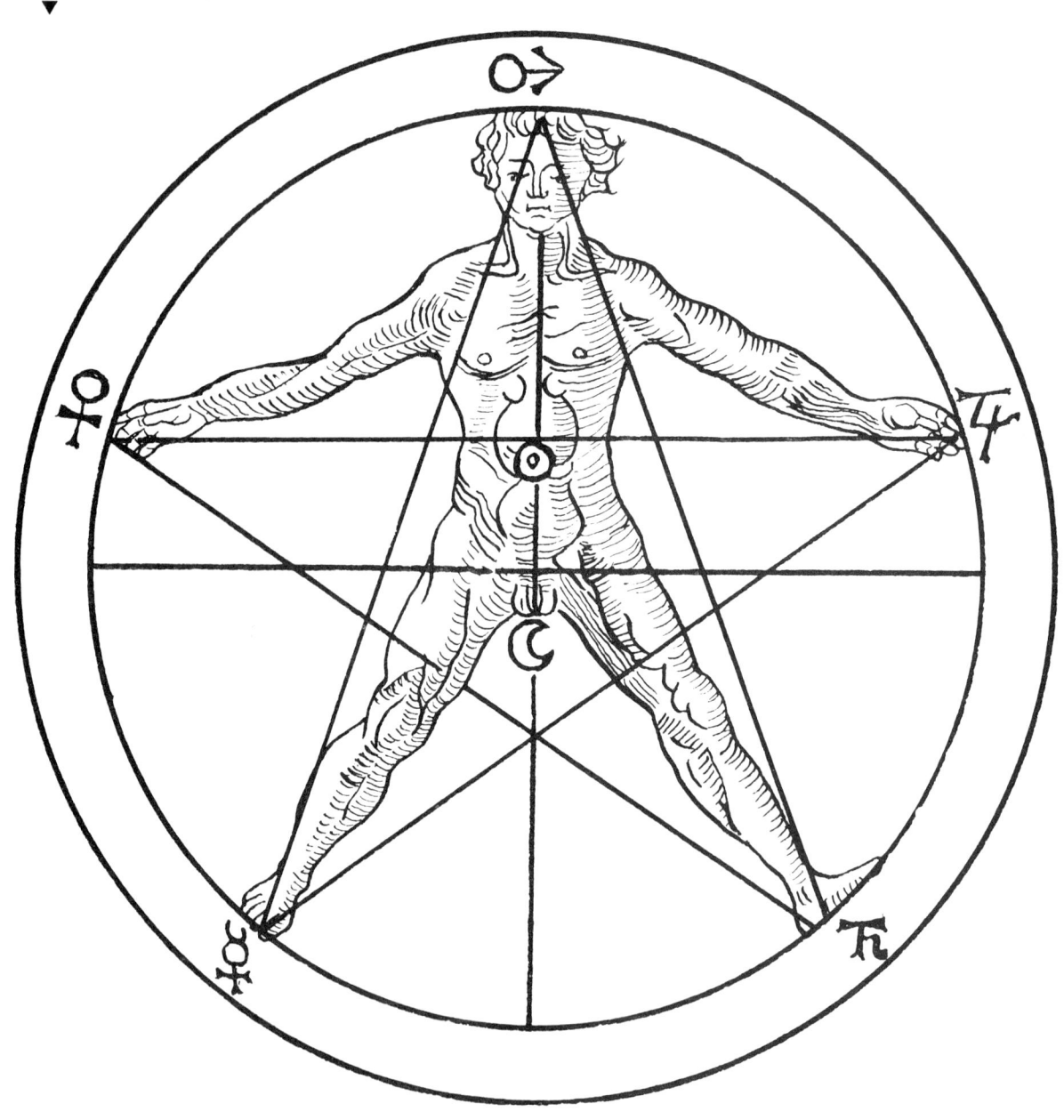

5
Predictions for the People, 1450-1700

We have seen how the philosophers, the writers and even royalty of the years 1450-1700 used astrology or reacted to its popularity. Now we can turn to look at astrology as it was practised in the context of everyday life, during the same centuries. This period is thought of as the peak of popularity for English astrology, and records show that a person from any walk of life, from a serving-maid to a great lady, could consult an astrologer.

The Astrologers

The most famous astrologer of the time was William Lilly, who was born in 1602, and lived to the ripe old age of seventy-nine. From his own writings and case-books, and from contemporary records, we can piece together a full and colourful account of his life.

Lilly came from humble origins, but came to London in 1620 and worked his way diligently through his early adult years, until, by marrying the widow of his deceased employer, he came into enough money to pursue his interests and hobbies as he wished. He soon developed an interest in astrology, and went for lessons to one John Arise Evans, a seedy practitioner living up an alley in the City of London. He was, said Lilly, "the most saturnine person my eyes ever beheld", notorious for his temper, being "very abusive and quarrelsome, seldom without a black eye". He seems to have given Lilly sound instruction in the art of casting horoscopes, but Lilly left him in disgust after he spotted Evans giving a false judgement to a client in order not to lose business.

Once Lilly began to practise in his own right, he had enormous success. It is estimated that he drew up to 2,000 charts in a year, and saw nearly as many clients. His customers came from all classes of society, and, by charging the rich as much as he could get away with, and the poor next to nothing, he pleased everyone and made himself a very good living. He was asked a multitude of different questions, all of which he had to try to solve through astrology. We find in his case-books, for instance, a merchant who asked whether his ship would come safely home from Spain, a tradesman who wished to know whether he could become rich without marrying, and a lady who was desperate to know whether her husband would be delivered from prison. (Yes, said Lilly, within three days.)

Lilly practised a great deal of horary astrology. He would draw up a chart for the time when the person consulted him, and interpret it by traditional rules, but with a great deal of personal skill and flair that many astrologers today wish they could equal! Many questions could be answered, but, as Lilly wrote in *Christian Astrology*, "judge not upon every trivial motion or light question, or when the querent has not the wit to know what he would demand". Horary astrology makes much use of the houses of the horoscope. The houses are a twelvefold division of the chart, based on the ascendant, which gives the beginning or "cusp" of the first house. Each house relates to different aspects of life. Questions of inheritance, for instance, were judged by Lilly from the eighth house, and if the two significators (relevant planets) were in opposition, then there would be "much wrangling" over the legacy.

He was asked countless questions about stolen goods, but these he had to treat with care, as it was against the law at that time to predict the whereabouts of thieves or their spoils. Lilly was accused of breaking the law several times, but he usually managed to extricate himself from the trouble. In his book *Christian Astrology* he gives precise guidelines for answering problems to do with theft. If you wish to know where the goods are, then look to the planet ruling the fourth house of the horoscope. If it is Saturn, aspected to Mars, look "about some dirty place, where people seldom go, a privy, etc". But if Venus, then try "a bed, or among bed-clothes, or where females much frequent". In a masterly analysis, on 10 February 1638, he interpreted a horoscope to find out who had stolen his own fish, which he had ordered for his Lent food. He decided that it was a bargeman, and of a particular type; he procured a warrant to search the house of the suspect, and, he says: "I found part of my fish in the water, part eaten, part not consumed; all confessed." Another time, he was asked to locate a lost dog by astrology. With extraordinary accuracy, he predicted that it would be found in an upstairs room in Long Acre (in London) next Monday. Sure enough, a friend of the dog's owner found the missing animal in just such a place, and "sent him home about ten o'clock on the Monday morning, to my very great credit".

38 John Evans, Lilly's teacher. ▶

◀ 37 William Lilly, perhaps England's best known astrologer. A portrait from the frontispiece of his almanack for 1678.

Bulfinch del.   Godfrey sc.

JOHN EVANS,

The Ill-favour'd Astrologer of Wales.

Engraved from the Original Drawing
In the Collection of the Right Hon[ble].
LORD CARDIFF.

Publish'd June 1st 1776 by F. Blyth No. 87 Cornhill.

There were many astrologers who could be consulted in London, and in other parts of England at the time. Not all were as reputable as Lilly; the "greatest skill" of one Alexander Hart, who lived in Houndsditch, "was to elect to young gentlemen fit times to play at Dice". Some, like William Hodges of Wolverhampton, combined astrology with the more occult practice of crystal-ball gazing. Horoscopes were drawn then in a square form, and remained in this shape until the twentieth century, when they became circular.

Simon Forman, born near Salisbury in 1552, was a well-known astrologer like Lilly, and, like him, was a self-made man from a poor background. He was interested in magic as well as in astrology, and kept a scrupulous diary, noting all his dreams, the day-to-day events of his life, and records of the people who sought him out to have horoscopes read. In one respect he was very different from Lilly; his great hobby was to seduce as many of his lady clients as possible, and, having done so, he would record the fact faithfully in his diary! It is considered that one woman with whom he had an affair may well be the "Dark Lady" of the series of sonnets by Shakespeare, based on the poet's love for a lady never identified. Simon also drew up charts for his own guidance; he was thinking of getting married, and cast a horary chart to discover whether the young lady he had in mind was suitable. Unfortunately not! The astrological answer was that "she will prove a whore".

Forman and Lilly both had a genuine interest in treating illness, and they used astrology to help diagnose and predict the course of diseases. Eventually, they were both allowed to practise properly as professional medical advisers, but not until they had encountered much difficulty. Forman faced opposition from the powerful Barber Surgeons, the body of men who carried out surgical operations, as well as from the Royal College of Physicians, who showed some professional jealousy in their dislike of this unlicensed, but popular and hard-working practitioner.

The most successful combination of astrology and medicine at the time was made by Nicholas Culpeper (1616-1664). His written work on the treatment of illness with herbs, *Culpeper's Complete Herbal*, has been popular ever since he wrote it, and sits on many bookshelves today. By then, the system of ascribing planetary rulers to each plant had become rather confused, and Culpeper produced a clear account of each herb, his opinion of its astrological significance, and its medical properties. To him, the study of astrology was an essential part of medicine. A physician without astrology, he said, is "like a lamp without oil".

Almanacks

One of the favourite forms of astrology at that time was the printed almanack, published in thousands and widely available. This was a kind of annual calendar, containing a wealth of information, based mainly on astrological forecasts. The customary way of beginning an almanack was to define the year for which it was written, by stating how many years had passed since God made the world, how many since he had given the promise to Abraham, and so on. Then followed each month of the year, complete with lunar phases, saints' days, and the astrological forecasts. Here is an extract from an almanack for 1683:

Note that four or five times is Mercury busy with the rest of the planets. His square to Saturn threatens Mechanics with lots of trade. . . . His sextile to Mars gives some of the ingenious soldiery preferment.

The effects of a comet were thought to last for the same number of years as the number of

39 and **40** (overleaf)   Two illustrations from an early almanack, one showing an eclipse, and the other the sign of Sagittarius.

In this present yere of .xlv. shall we haue an Eclypse of the Sonne, beyng great nearhand iiii. poyntes. And the begynnynge therof shall be the .ix. daye of June, at .vii. of the clocke, and .lii. minutes before noon. The mydde of the Eclypse at .viii. of the clocke, and .xl. minutes. The ende therof at .ix. of the clocke, and .xxviii. minutes. This Eclypse shall last an houre and an half. And this Eclypse shall gyue his influence and operacyon this yeare, by reason of his distaunce from the orientall corner.

agittarius is a watery signe manly, meane ☉ of the day, & cauſeth man fayrer behynde than before, ſlender here a greate belly, a longe viſage, & a ſlender chynne.

1   d   Libra 11
2   e   libra 26
3   f   wenefrede   Scor 8
4   g   Amande conf pius 21

The newe moon the, iiii, day at, ii, the clocke, xxxv, minu, after noone, colde with turbacyon,

5   a   Letus preſt   Sagit 4
6   b   Leonarde   tarius 18
7   c   wilbrord byſ Capri 2
8   Of the tribut cor 16
9   e   peny, mat, xxii, nus 30
10   f   Martyn con Aqua 15
11   g   Martin byſh rius 29

The fyrſt quarter the, xi, day at, i, the clocke after noon, drye, yet wyndy,

41 A fifteenth-century woodcut from a very popular almanack called the *Shepherd's Calendar*. The month of July, ruled by Cancer and Leo, is shown here, with the harvest in progress.

As the almanacks were bought and read extensively by country folk, they contained monthly gardening and farming notes, rather as one would expect to find a gardener's column in the newspaper today, but with the difference that the planetary positions were taken into account as much as the seasons:

Geld sheep and other cattle, the Moon in Aries, Sagittarius, or Capricorn, being in her last quarter, benignly configured, and free from the realms of Saturn and Mars.

We have the names and histories of many of the almanack-makers of the day; some of them called themselves by such grand titles as "Student of the physical celestial sciences", and even Lilly named himself "Merlinus Anglicus". Competition was fierce, and the rival astrologers slandered each other venomously through their publications, and pamphlets printed specially for the purpose. George Wharton, Lilly's contemporary, was his greatest rival, and poured scorn on his predictions, calling him "that juggling wizard, William Lilly . . . a fellow made up of nothing but mischief, tautologies, and barbarism". But the astrologers forgot their differences when they gathered for the great Astrologers' Feasts. Here, those who normally fought over professional matters, politics and religion, could put aside their quarrels for the evening and enjoy themselves, probably picking up some good astrological tips from each other into the bargain.

The astrologers and the almanack-makers used their art to make political predictions, and to pronounce on the future welfare of the country. This could be dangerous, as Lilly found out. Some years before the Great Fire of London, in 1666, which was followed by an outbreak of plague, he had published some "hieroglyphical figures" which were supposed to relate to the future of London. One of them showed twins (representing Gemini, the sign which rules

days for which the comet was visible; hence, once a comet had made its appearance, it was usually good material for astrological predictions for several years afterwards. "Many battles and sharp conflicts both by sea and land, unusual storms and tempests, unnatural barrenness of the earth" were forecast as a consequence of a comet that appeared in Easter week, 1677.

Many of the almanack-writers fancied themselves as poets, and put even their astrological weather-forecasts into verse:

Venus and Mercury in the Cancer meet,
With hasty showers the Hay-Maker doth let:
They both apply to Mars, sometimes threat rain,
But Sol and Hermes* clear the air again.

*Sun and Mercury

London), upside-down and surrounded by flames. Men with buckets of water were trying to quench the fire. Lilly had also said that he feared a terrible calamity for London which would come about through "sundry fires and a consuming plague". Now, when the fire did take place, his accurate predictions did not bring him applause, for he was summoned before a committee to prove that he had not started the fire himself! In the uneasy political climate which followed the disturbed years of Civil War in England, this was not such an unlikely accusation. Lilly seems to have had a lucky horoscope himself, for he came off lightly and was not charged with the offence.

42 A typical page from an almanack. The left-hand page gives saints' days and planetary positions; the right sets out some bold predictions.
▼

The Decline of Astrology

At the time of its greatest popularity, the seeds of decline were already present for astrology. The almanacks continued to sell in great numbers, and new ones were published — but some of these were satires on the serious predictions. Like the proper almanacks, they make delightful and amusing reading. The first known English parody, entitled *A Merry Prognostication*, published in 1554, reads:

But I say if the ninth day of November
Had fallen upon the tenth day of December
It had been a marvellous hot year for bees
For then the Moon had been like a green
  cheese.

In his almanack for 1678, *Merlini Anglici*, Lilly had argued that a margin of error was acceptable in an astrologer's work:

Is not an error in the astrologer as tolerable as in the Divine, Physician or Lawyer. . . . Does the Physician always cure?

But witty "Poor Robin" (the pseudonym of another parodying almanack-writer) jested on:

*Thus you have each month's
  Prognostication
Of many things may happen in this nation
And we as true as others guess in this
Some of them sure may happen, and some
  miss;
For there is in our art of skill so little,
We can't hit everything unto a tittle.*

By the close of the seventeenth century there was as much laughter as serious interest surrounding astrology. The writer Jonathan Swift published a fake almanack in 1707, supposedly by an Isaac Bickerstaff, in which he predicted that one of the most famous almanack-writers of the time, John Partridge, would die "upon the 29th of March next, about eleven at night, of a raging fever". Following this date, he went on to print an account of the poor man's supposed death! Partridge lost no time in proclaiming that he was alive and well, and that it had been a hoax, but he was much mocked, and indeed the Stationer's Company took it all seriously, struck his name off their register, and left him without a licence to print for several years.

Astrology was losing its appeal. The public, flooded with many carelessly-produced, poorly-written almanacks, began to think of astrology as old-fashioned. Learned men turned their attention to the new discoveries of science. It was left to a very few to carry astrology through until its revival in the nineteenth century.

44 "Poor Robin" almanack – mocking the conventional publications. Note that his list of saints' days is far from orthodox!

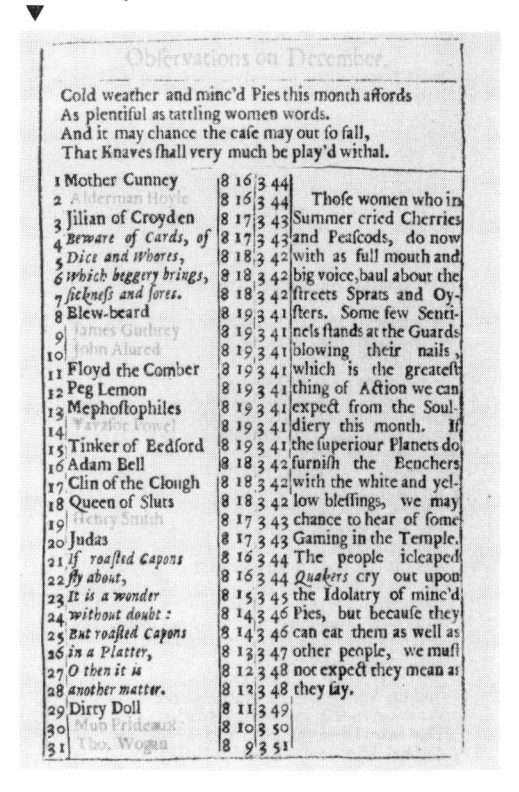

43 Lilly's famous picture, which earned him the credit and the suspicion of having predicted the Great Fire of London. The twins represent Gemini, the sign which rules London.

6
Astrology at Low Ebb, 1700-1850

By the beginning of the eighteenth century the tide of English astrology, which had flowed so exuberantly fifty years earlier, was now receding to a low ebb. All over Europe, astrology lost its respectability, and scarcely survived at all at this period. But survive it did, and in England alone. A succession of astrologers and writers kept the tradition alive in Britain after it had disappeared from notice on the Continent.

The reasons why astrology fell into disfavour are several, and some have been mentioned already — the "loss" of an earth-centred universe, and the discrediting of the profession by bogus astrologers. Additionally, in the eighteenth and nineteenth centuries, the attitude to science changed radically. It had been regarded as a field of learning which could incorporate religious and philosophical elements, but now men tried to rid it of anything that could be called superstition. If something could not be weighed, or measured, or proved by mathematical law, then it was suspect. Because of this highly rational and practical approach, science, medicine, and industry made great progress, but traditions which were not wholly based on material law were pushed to one side. For practical matters, of course, a scientist needs facts and figures that he can rely on. No one wants to employ an electrician who is unsure of the strength of the current that he is using! But it can be argued that our experience is not merely made up of facts and figures, and that man has an emotional and a spiritual side to his experience which he can learn about, but which cannot be measured in exactly the same way as one measures the speed of light or the weight of a brick. Many people today feel that the progress of the last 250 years or so has neglected this side of life.

Astrology does not fit readily into a scientific category, for it is based on the idea that every event and birth is marked by a unique planetary pattern. No horoscope will ever be completely identical to any other, and so the exact effects of the overall pattern cannot be scientifically stated. Nor do most astrologers claim that their art is completely precise or reliable in its predictions, for the country that a man lives in, his family background, and his own strength of will will influence the way his horoscope works out.

By the eighteenth century astrology had become associated with superstition and fraudulent magic. A comedy called *The Astrologer*, published in 1744, ridicules astrology and those who believe in it. The villains — who rejoice in such names as Stargaze, Siftem, Sly and Brag — plan to defraud a gullible man called Doterel, who is a great believer in astrology. "You shall see that ev'n Astrology, an old, exploded cheat, by the force of unintelligible cant and magisterial grimace, will bring us in more profit than all the arts and sciences together", claims the ringleader gleefully. The greedy tricksters persuade Doterel to place absurd amounts of gold and jewels in a room so that, by planetary magic, Jupiter, who rules over wealth, will be pleased to grant Doterel his request. ("Jupiter must have a distinct offering; and being a sovereign planet, delights in nothing but money, ready money.") Indeed, Doterel is foolish enough to offer 999 guineas in gold to the planetary deity. Predictably enough, the treasure mysteriously disappears during the phoney ritual, stolen by the bogus astrologers.

Although astrology had lost the respect of the upper classes, it continued to keep some of its popularity among the working folk. A few almanacks were still published, bought and consulted. One, the *Vox*

45 In 1620 John Melton published a scathing attack on astrology in a book called *The Astrologaster*, of which this is the title page. Melton called astrology an "art, whereby cunning knaves cheat plain honest men", and describes what he sees as a typical visit to an astrologer, who is found "before a square table, covered with a green carpet, on which lay a huge book . . . full of strange characters; . . . not far from that . . . all the superstitious or rather fained instruments of his cousening (deceiving) art".
▼

▲
46 Ebenezer Sibly — a portrait set into a horoscope. He has the sign of Gemini ascending, which means that producing copious pages of writing is very natural to him!

▲
47 A page from Sibly's book. The horoscope (held by an angel!) shows America's declaration of Independence.

Stellarum, was printed in huge numbers at this time: in 1768 nearly 107,000 copies were sold. A few practitioners lingered on. In about 1750 a Mr Creighton was known to have practised professional astrology and saw his clients "a few doors from Ludgate-Hill, on the right hand side of the way". We also have records of a rarer type of astrologer at that time — a lady professional, known as Mrs Williams. She courted a better class of client by plying her trade at the fashionable gathering places such as Bath. She advertised herself as available to ladies only "from ten in the morning until eight in the evening".

To begin with, the astrological writings of this period were few and far between, and were mostly re-writes of sixteenth-century texts. Ebenezer Sibly (1752-1799), who took over a thousand pages to expound the *Complete Illustration of the Celestial Art of Astrology*, is considered to have added nothing new to the tradition whatsoever. However, such books did keep astrological instruction available for anyone who was interested. John Worsdale (1766-1826) was more original, and gave juicy examples from his own case histories, but showed an attitude in his work which would horrify today's astrologers. Apparently, he took great delight in predicting the time and manner of death for the clients whose horoscopes he drew up. He told a Mary Dickson that she would not marry; she retorted that he was wrong, since she was already engaged. He added that something of "an awful nature" would happen before the wedding date, which would cause death by water. Although the young lady appears to have taken his prediction lightly at the time, the following spring she fell from a boat and was drowned. Very few responsible astrologers give predictions as to the time of death;

besides the fact that such a prediction must always be uncertain, such a pronouncement can cause great distress and even harm to the person.

There was one believer in astrology during the eighteenth century who is set in a category quite of her own. This is Lady Lucy Hester Stanhope, the niece of the prominent English statesman William Pitt (1708-1788). From the start Hester was a wilful and unconventional girl, who rebelled against the strict social rules governing women, encouraged her brother to run away from home, and delighted in tackling life in her own way. As a young woman, she looked after Pitt for a long time, and enjoyed being so close to the source of political power when he was in office. After his death she grew dissatisfied with England, and set off abroad, where she remained to the end of her days. She travelled extensively in the Middle East, survived shipwreck and plague, and eventually made her home near Mount Lebanon. At first, her companions had feared for her life, for she insisted on riding out alone, unveiled, through Arab towns, which was the most unseemly behaviour possible for a lady in those countries. Perhaps her actions were so outrageous that she was thought of as a woman apart, for she came to be loved and respected by the natives, and was often known as "Queen".

It is not known how she learnt her astrology, and indeed it seems that it was based partly upon intuition. She plainly understood some conventional theory, but did not draw up horoscopes herself. Visitors to her Middle Eastern home soon found that she was an expert at reading people's character from their faces, in which she could, she said, discern traces of their ruling planet and hence their essential nature. She kept faith with the old system of planetary correspondences, believing that each planet would rule over a series of plants, animals and so on, and that a man would share the preferences of his ruling star. In conversation with her physician, she said:

> *Every star has attached to it two aerial beings, two animals, two trees, two flowers etc, that is a couple of all the grand classes in creation, animal, vegetable, mineral or etherial, whose antipathies and sympathies become congenial with the being born under the same star. . . . My brother, Charles, vomited if he eat three strawberries only . . . other people, born under the same star as his, may not have such an insurmountable antipathy as his was, because their star may be imperfect, while his was pure. . . .*

(From *The Memoirs of Lady Lucy Hester Stanhope*)

◄48 Sir William Herschel (1738–1822). He lived in England for most of his life.

Just as astrology looked fit to disappear for ever, it slowly began to regain ground in the popular imagination. But as it did so, it had to take account of two startling discoveries. In 1781 an amateur astronomer called Herschel saw a "star" through his telescope that could not possibly be a star. It was proved to be another planet in our solar system. At first, the new planet was called Herschel, but soon the name Uranus was adopted, that of the Greek and Roman god of the heavens. In 1846 yet another planet was discovered, and was named Neptune, after the god of the sea. Gone was the sacred number seven of the "planets" of the horoscope — Sun, Moon, Mercury, Venus, Mars, Jupiter and Saturn. Now there were an uneasy nine, though this was later to be rounded up to a symbolically more satisfactory ten with the discovery of Pluto in the twentieth century. But astrology absorbed the news calmly, and soon began to try out meanings for the new planets.

The law still frowned on astrologers. In 1824 the famous Vagrancy Act was passed, designed to punish "incorrigible rogues" who might be roaming the street or parish. This included convicts, pedlars, prostitutes and tramps, all of whom are mentioned specifically in the act. Unfortunately for the respectable practitioners of astrology, the act also contained a clause that "every Person pretending or professing to tell Fortunes" should be included. Strictly speaking, therefore, professional astrology was now illegal, although the interpretation of the law was open to much dispute. It was applied at times; a Francis Copestick advertised his services in his own almanack,

50   The title page for *The Astrologer of the Nineteenth Century*.

49   An artist's impression of Herschel discovering Uranus. Although the scene shown is one of excitement at the discovery, this is really very unlikely, as Herschel did not at first realize what it was that he had spotted. At first, he thought it might be a comet, but after much further work and calculation he was at last able to prove that it was a new planet.

THE ASTROLOGER,
of the Nineteenth Century,
OR THE
Master Key of Futurity,
being a Complete System of
ASTROLOGY, GEOMANCY & OCCULT SCIENCE.

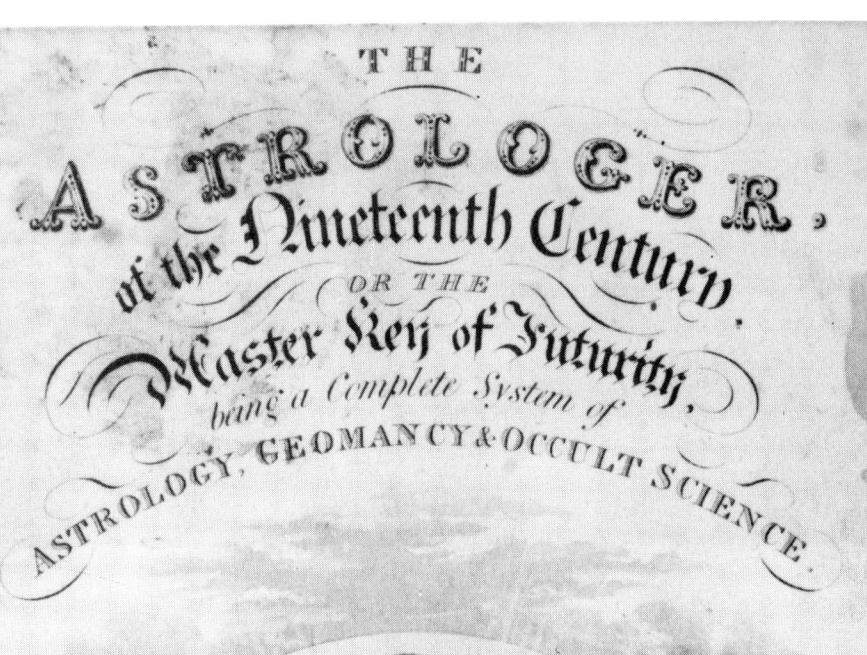

I consider the heavens the work of thy fingers, the Moon and the Stars, which thou hast ordained. Psal. VIII. 3.

They fought from heaven, the Stars in their courses fought against Sisera. Judges v. 20.

Sidus adsit amicum. Cicero.

and was visited by plain clothes officers who arrested him after they had paid him to do a horoscope. Although such arrests appear to have been the exception rather than the rule, they were a constant threat to astrologers and caused much anger among them.

The rise of astrology into favour again may be traced through the course of magazines published from the late eighteenth century onwards. The first to specialize in astrology had the inappropriate title of *The Conjuror's Magazine*, first published in 1791. William Gilbert, who wrote articles for it, also offered private lessons in the art of talisman-making. He obviously valued his ability highly: "I will be ... PAID and paid HANDSOMELY," he said, and set his fees at between £20 and £150 per year,

staggeringly high charges for those days. Another magazine, *Urania*, did not, alas, do so well. It only ran to one issue, and a note handwritten by the editor on a copy confesses that he was sadly let down by those who promised him help with it, and, for want of correspondents, had written the letter page himself!

A better known figure in the astrological world was Robert Cross Smith, who chose the celestial name of Raphael to write under. He started a new almanack, called the *Prophetic Messenger*, which did so well, that it was continued by a succession of "Raphaels" after his death. Even today, Raphael's annual ephemeris, giving the planetary positions for every day, is a standard reference work. Smith also brought out a new magazine, called *The Straggling Astrologer*. It only survived a few months, but after its demise, he rebound the remaining copies with some additional material, and sold it in book form as *The Astrologer of the Nineteenth Century*. Printed in 1825, it makes marvellous reading. It is full of

51 A dramatic illustration from *The Astrologer of the Nineteenth Century*, showing all the awful omens accompanying the death of Lord Byron, the poet. Byron died on 19 April 1824.
▼

REVIEW OF THE OMENS BY WHICH THE DEATH OF LORD BYRON WAS PREFIGURED.

54

sensational stories of apparitions and hauntings, and horoscopes drawn up to explain the causes of various disasters. The reader may find out why Mr Harris failed to ascend in his balloon, why the Amphion of War was blown up at Plymouth, and why Lord Byron met his end. Instructions are given, accompanied by lurid illustrations, for making planetary talismans. One, said to have

52 The title page of Zadkiel's magazine.
▼

ZADKIEL'S MAGAZINE,

OR

RECORD AND REVIEW

OF

ASTROLOGY, PHRENOLOGY, MESMERISM,

AND OTHER SCIENCES.

O MAGNA VIS VERITATIS!

VOL. I.]   JANUARY 1849.   [No. 1.

CONTENTS.

	Page
On the present State and future Prospects of Astrology, with some Account of its Origin, &c.	1
Aurora Borealis	9
Mesmerism in India forty Years ago, by Col. Bagnold	12
Astrology and the Press	16
Reviews:—The Poetry of Science—The Gem of the Astral Sciences	24
Meteorology	26
The Planet Neptune, Theory of Astro-Meteorology	28
Aphorisms touching Weather, Meteors, &c. by J. Cardan	29
Unfilled Predictions	30
Great Earthquake, &c.	31
Remarkable and Unfortunate Nativity	32

LONDON: HALL & CO., 25, PATERNOSTER ROW,
AND SOLD BY ALL BOOKSELLERS.

Price Sixpence.

the property of destroying insects, is given with the following recommendation:

The manuscript from which this is taken cost 50 guineas, and a medical gentleman, to whom it belonged, affirms that he had himself proved the truth of this observation; for being at one time much annoyed with beetles, he made this talisman, and screwed it to the floor, when these troublesome insects immediately disappeared.

Among the lively, but more doubtful accounts, are some quite sound pieces of astrological advice and instruction, such as how to cast a natal chart, how to interpret planetary aspects and so on — all based on tradition but with valuable insights which are still useful today. The reader should not be led to think, from the contributions by the so-called Princess Olive of Cumberland, that an interest was taken by royalty; Princess Olive was, in fact, one Mrs Olivia Serres, whose claim to be the daughter of the Duke of Cumberland was never officially recognized!

Astrology was slowly spreading through the upper classes of society once more, but was still of doubtful reputation. Lieutenant James Morrison, a respected naval officer, who moved in the best circles, called himself Zadkiel, and began a rival almanack to Raphael's. He kept the two worlds separate, however; he did not like his astrological activities to be guessed at by his aristocratic acquaintances, and suffered some social disgrace when they became public knowledge.

England had kept astrological tradition alive in its most barren period. In the twentieth century, there was to be a tremendous resurgence of interest in astrology, both at home and abroad, and important new developments were to come from astrologers working both in Europe and in the USA.

7
The Road Leads On — Astrology from 1850 to the Present Day

Until the twentieth century the astrologer's lot could be a lonely one. Astrology in the eyes of the world was no better than street fortune-telling, or a superstitious relic from the past. Perhaps the astrologers deserved this opinion to some extent, for they had been content to rely upon old books and methods without question. Although the basis of astrology is so ancient, it can only stay alive if it is constantly up-dated with new ideas and approaches. As the twentieth century drew near, there was a fresh stirring of interest, and a genuine attempt to put astrology into terms that a modern man could understand.

One of the earliest figures in this revival was Richard Garnett, who lived from 1835–1906, and was Keeper of Printed Books at the British Museum. Unlike so many of his predecessors, he was not content to use the old descriptions of astrology, but did experimental work of his own. One of his research projects was to try to find out what planets were associated with mental illness, and he wrote up his results under the pseudonym of A.G. Trent (an anagram of his real name!) Perhaps even he was uncertain of the effect it would have on his professional reputation

53 A comic portrait of Richard Garnett, a ▶ scholarly astrologer. (From *Prominent Men, 1880–1910* by H. Furniss.)

if it were known that he was interested in such a "cranky" subject.

And then the boom started. In 1878 a London branch of the Theosophical Society was formed. This was an organization which had been founded in New York a few years earlier, and was headed internationally by Helena Blavatsky, an extraordinary woman who claimed to have produced a true synthesis of ancient religious teachings. Theosophy means "divine wisdom", and its followers placed great emphasis on mystical experience, and on seeking out the hidden or "esoteric" meaning at the core of different religious traditions. The activities of the society inspired its members — of whom there were many — to study and search out all kinds of occult and spiritual knowledge, both in Eastern teachings, such as Hinduism and Buddhism, and closer to home in some of the ancient Western traditions, such as astrology. The Theosophical Society became a focus for those seeking to know more about astrology, and in due course a special Astrological Lodge was set up as part of the Society, to give facilities for the exchange of astrological ideas and teachings. The Lodge still thrives today, and keeps a very high standard of lectures and classes.

Another occult society arose — more secretive than the Theosophical Society in its activities — with a membership that included many famous names of the period, such as Algernon Blackwood, the writer, and W.B. Yeats, the poet. This was the Order of the Golden Dawn, whose initiates were taught symbolism and magic. The society was highly structured and members had to pass exams to be promoted from one grade to the next. To join was to take on a heavy commitment, and involved a lot of work. Members painted complex geometrical symbols, learnt the Hebrew names of God, practised solemn ritual, and made magical weapons that had to be precise in every detail. They had to practise a method of divination, and the tradition of astrology was one that was commonly learnt. W.B. Yeats wove much of the magical symbolism of the Golden Dawn into his writings, and here and there he talks about astrology in specific terms:

There is an astrological sense in which a man's wife or sweetheart is always an Eve made from a rib of his body. She is drawn to him because she represents a group of stellar influences in the radical horoscope.... Whether this element be good or evil, she is therefore its external expression.
(From *Estrangement*)

By now, there were also people keen to practise astrology who did not belong to any special sect or group. In 1887 a new magazine was founded: *The Astrologer*. It cost only 2d, and set out to present easy lessons in astrology to its readers. To the editor's surprise, he was soon receiving an enthusiastic fan mail, with many letters from readers who already knew some astrology, clamouring for more advanced articles. The magazine announced that private lessons would also be available for those who wanted to get ahead faster than the lessons in the magazine could take them. These, with charts, were to cost 2s 7d. Correspondents were delighted with the good value offered to them: "Professional astrologers seem to be so reticent and charge so heavy for any little information they give...."; "About 14 years ago, a friend of mine in Lancashire paid *five* or *six* pounds for a few written lessons on astrology." They enthused over the magazine's contents, and appealed for it to be more widely available: "We must have it on W.H. Smith's bookstalls"!

The editor, Mr P. Powley, began an astrological problem page for which readers were invited to send in their queries, enclosing, of course, the appropriate birth data. The page makes a refreshing change to the problem pages that we see in women's magazines today:

No. 2.   Entered at Stationers' Hall.

The Astrologer.
AUG., 1887.

THE NATIVITY

2D. MONTHLY. 2D.
H. VICKERS, 317, STRAND, LONDON, W.C.

"Constant Reader" — The description of the person with whom you will share your lot, is one of medium height, neat, clean and well-composed; of a pleasant expression, oval visage, rather light hair, possessing a good disposition, and is much respected.

After a few years the editor was no longer able to continue, and a man named William Frederick Allen agreed to take the magazine over. Allen became famous under the pseudonym of Alan Leo, and was the key writer of the early twentieth century. He produced a series of astrological text books which meant that reasonably-priced, up-to-date astrological manuals were now within the reach of the general public. He was a Theosophist, and his books carry the flavour of this. Nevertheless, despite his high spiritual ideals, he was not averse to making a good living out of astrology, and at one time was running what was virtually a horoscope factory. He and his employees sent out to eager customers a "personal" interpretation of their horoscope, much of which, in fact consisted of duplicated material.

Eventually, British newspapers and magazines woke up to the fact that astrology was popular and might go down well with their readers. In 1930 the *Sunday Express* began a regular astrology column. This was written by R.H. Naylor, who became a very famous astrologer. He scored an early success when he predicted imminent danger for British aircraft, and shortly afterwards the R101 airship crashed on its maiden flight. Since then, newspaper astrology has never looked back. Most columns are, of course, greatly simplified in astrological terms, since their predictions are based on sunsigns only. Many serious astrologers today dislike the complex art of astrology being reduced to this level, and call such journalistic astrology nonsense. Others see it as a useful way of keeping the public interested in astrology; after all, if it had not been for the popular almanacks of earlier days, astrology might have died out long ago.

In the Second World War astrology was put to a more sinister use. It was suspected that Karl Ernst Krafft, a Swiss astrologer, was advising Hitler in his campaigns. The Nazis had alread tried to use new interpretations of Nostradamus as propaganda in their favour. (Nostradamus was a sixteenth-century astrologer and clairvoyant who phrased his predictions in a very ambiguous way.) So the British Intelligence employed a counter-agent astrologer, Louis de Wohl, who was commissioned to work out what kind of astrological advice Hitler might be receiving. Another job given to him was to make up and publish some fake issues of a real German astrological magazine, *Zenit*, to be distributed on enemy territory, and containing bogus predictions designed to sabotage Germany's actions. For instance, the magazine suggested suitable days for U-boats to put to sea or to stay at home.

After the war, the expansion of astrology continued, with some excellent astrologers emerging. For example, there was Charles Carter (1887–1968), who wrote several clear and helpful books. One, the *Encyclopedia of Psychological Astrology*, is quite unusual, giving the results of Carter's research into "case histories", where he tried to find out what special factors in a horoscope would produce various personality traits or illnesses. Opening the book at "F", for instance, we find such headings as "Foulness of Speech", "Frankness", "Fraud", "Friendliness", "Frugality" and "Fussiness" discussed.

In 1958 the Astrological Association was founded, to provide a more broadly-based association, without ties to one particular line of teaching, as was the case with the Astrological Lodge which retained its strong links with the Theosophical Society. The Astrological Association is now a very large organization, with a membership of both pro-

◀54 The title page of *The Astrologer*, a magazine whose success astonished its editor.

▲
55 Alan Leo. With four planets in the sign of Leo in his natal horoscope, he had no trouble in choosing his pen-name.

fessional and amateur astrologers. Although we *can* split up the astrological world into professionals and amateurs, it can be misleading to do so. The amateur astrologer can range from someone who has merely read a couple of books on the subject, and enjoys trying to guess what his friends' sun-signs are, to a person who has studied it in depth over many years, but does not make a living from it. Members of the Astrological Association can share information on research, horoscope interpretation, and current astro-

56 Charles Carter, an astrologer whose work is much read and respected today.

logical theories through the Association's journal, regular meetings and data files.

Today, books and tuition in astrology are widely available. In England there are two organizations which give correspondence courses in astrology for those who wish to learn in a highly disciplined and thorough manner. These are the Faculty of Astrological Studies and the Jeff Mayo School of Astrology. Their courses lead to certificates and diplomas, and the examinations to gain these awards are conducted rigorously.

However, there are many who do not feel the need of a qualification to practise astrology, whether for their own pleasure or professionally. These people can learn from friends, local groups, or even from Adult Education evening classes on astrology, which are now available in a number of areas.

Each year, an Astrological Conference is held in England and is attended by several hundred people. Anyone who believes that astrology is practised mainly by ladies bearing crystal balls and wearing long flowing robes, would be surprised to meet a cross-section of the participants! Scientists, teachers, artists, astronomers, businessmen and psychologists can all usually be found.

It would not be fair to imply that astrology is generally accepted by all scientists and professionals. Many express surprise and dismay that a tradition which they see as primitive superstition should continue to exist. In 1975, an attack against astrology was launched by Bart J. Bok, an American professor of astronomy, and printed in *The Humanist* magazine (Vol 35, no 5). It was made in the form of a statement denouncing astrology, and it was signed by 186 leading scientists, including Konrad Lorenz, B.F. Skinner, Fred Hoyle and Francis Crick. They announced that:

We ... wish to caution the public against the unquestioning acceptance of the predictions and advice given privately and publicly by astrologers. Those who wish to believe in astrology should realize that there is no scientific foundation for its tenets.... We believe that the time has come to challenge directly, and forcefully, the pretentious claims of astrological charlatans.

These same scientists are not without critics themselves, however. It has been said that their own attitude is not necessarily objective, that their attack upon astrology is based on a wish to see it refuted, rather

THE FACE OF ASTROLOGY

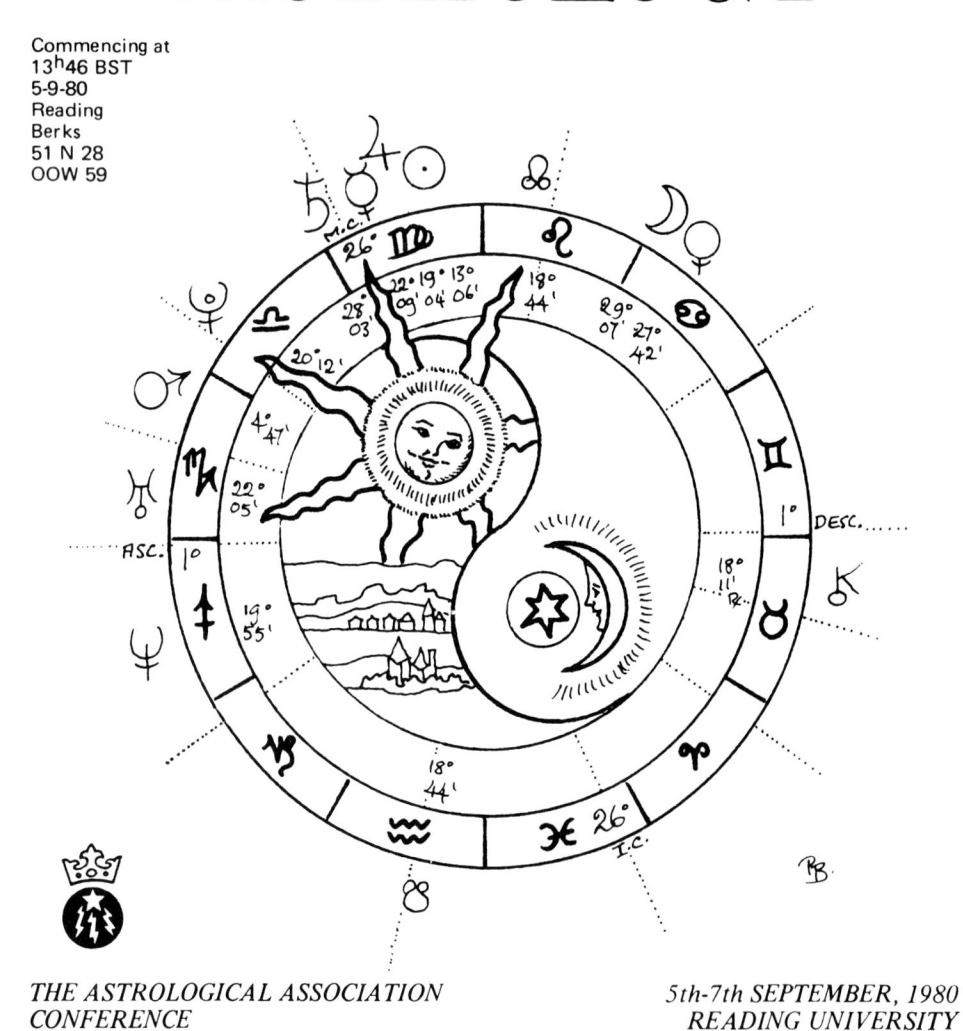

Commencing at
13h46 BST
5-9-80
Reading
Berks
51 N 28
OOW 59

THE ASTROLOGICAL ASSOCIATION   5th-7th SEPTEMBER, 1980
CONFERENCE   READING UNIVERSITY

The first time ever I saw your face,
  I thought the Sun rose in your eyes,
And the Moon and the Stars were the gifts you gave
  To the dark and the empty skies,
    My Love.

(Ewan MacColl)

than being an open approach to the subject which considers both sides of the question carefully before coming to any conclusion. Many people who have taken up astrology are themselves well-respected in academic and even scientific fields and it seems unlikely that they should all be victims of delusion and superstition.

Astrologers still meet with resistance in legal areas too. Although, today, the prohibition on fortune-telling in the Vagrancy Act has been repealed, it has been directly replaced with the Fraudulent Mediums Act of 1951 which makes it an offence to use telepathic or clairvoyant powers with intent to deceive. This does not implicate astrology as such, since the backbone of astrology is a skilled technique rather than telepathy. But many newspapers, out of excessive caution or perhaps ignorance, fear that someone placing an advertisement for astrology may be "fraudulent" in terms of the law, and so they refuse to take such advertisements.

◀ 57 The cover of the programme for the Astrological Conference held in 1980 at Reading University.

▲
58 At such conferences, research can go on in between lectures. Here, a group of people who all have the same ascendant meet to be photographed. Their common sign is Capricorn, and they appear to fit well into the classical description of this sign as lean and serious in appearance, with a firm jaw and well-defined features.

Astrologers disagree among themselves as to how astrology works, and to what extent it is reliable. Some would like to see astrology "proved" in the same way as the exact sciences, to gain respectability in the modern world, and they carry out research with that aim in mind. Strangely enough, the most convincing evidence that astrology can be "proved" statistically, in some respects anyway, comes from a non-astrologer, Michel Gauquelin. When he analysed the horoscopes of thousands of sports champions, he found that far more of them have Mars placed just above the ascendant than could come about by chance. He has also shown that other planets may be prominent in a similar way when other professions are involved.

If astrology is to thrive, it is important that there should be debate, research, the testing of new methods and theories. Some will survive the test of time, others will not, but they all provide impetus and life. One new theory developed in England by John Addey is the technique of "planetary harmonics", based on the "harmonic wave" relationships between planets in the zodiac circle. This enables astrologers to work with more complex planetary interrelationships in each horoscope, and to draw out factors from the chart not immediately apparent by traditional methods. Another new theory, in the process of being developed by a group of Manchester astrologers, takes the astrological framework out beyond the solar system to include the Galactic Plane as well.

Astrology today is not confined to the study of personal horoscopes, although that is still the central focus. There are many fields in which astrology has been used with interesting, and often successful results. Over many years John Nelson investigated the relationship between planetary positions and radio disturbance; he came up with a series of particular aspects between planets which appeared to relate to this disturbance, and was able to forecast such "radio storms" with impressive accuracy.

▲
59　John Addey (born 1920), a leading figure in astrological research.

Other lines of research have included the relationship of astrology to plant growth, earthquakes, stockmarket cycles, and weather-forecasting. Nowadays all forms of astrological research have been greatly helped by the arrival of the computer, particularly since these have become widely available to business firms and private individuals. Not only statistical calculations, but also astrological chart erection can be done on the computer. This can save endless time when complicated astrological techniques are being used, or hundreds of horoscopes compared. However, the temptation to interpret horoscopes via the computer has crept in, and one can buy a computer-produced astrological profile for very little these days. Those who take the tradition seriously would say that the horoscope requires a person of experience and understanding to interpret it. After all, few of us would trust ourselves to a computer rather than to a doctor to diagnose and prescribe for us!

Astrology in England is flourishing. It exists on many levels, from the popular and superficial, to the learned and serious. Today's astrologers are adventurous and forward-looking, and are taking their knowledge into the fields of science, medicine, psychology and self-development. Astrology has led a life of ups and downs, sometimes the stuff of everyday life, sometimes of obscurity; it has survived scientific change and hard-line religious examination, and still, in our space-age century, lives to fascinate yet another generation. The ancient symbols, familiar, yet mysterious, hold us yet.

The Ram, the Bull, the Heavenly Twins
And next the Crab the Lion shines,
The Virgin and the Scales,
The Scorpion, Archer, and Sea-Goat
The Man that bears the Watering Pot
The Fishes' glittering tails.
(Anon)

BIRTH CHART

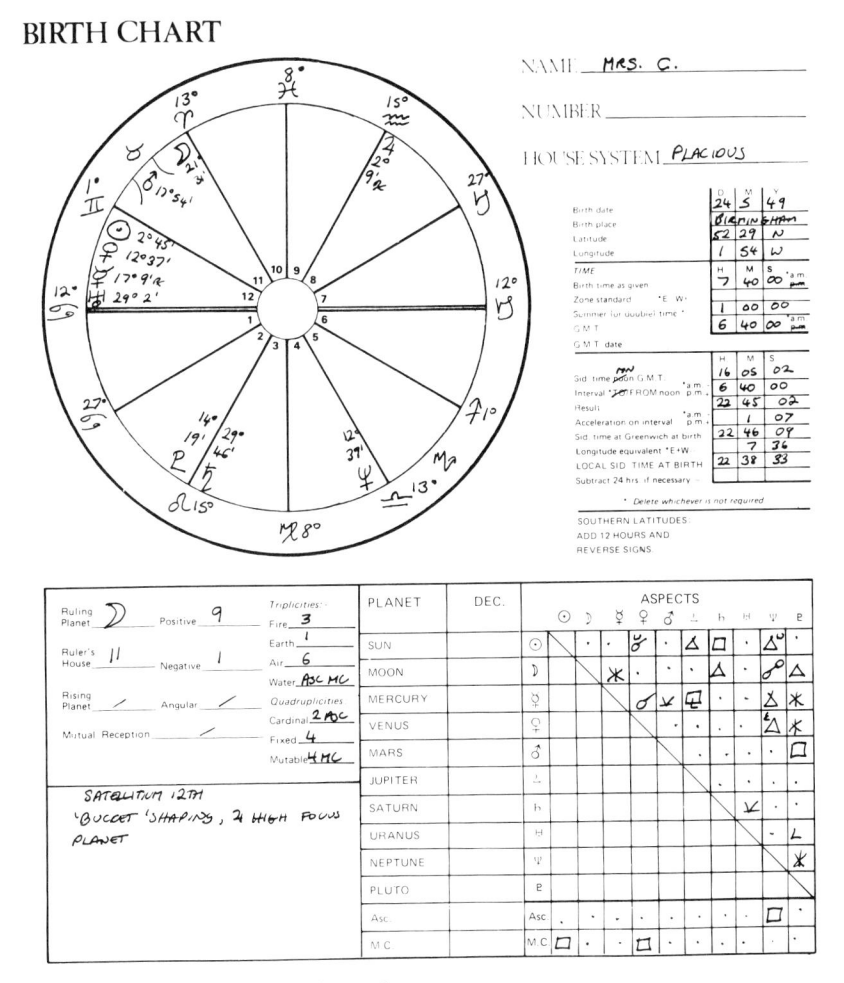

▲
60 A modern horoscope, drawn up by the author.

Date List

c. 3,000 BC	First written texts on astrology which have survived from Babylon.
c. 2,800 BC	Construction of first stage of Stonehenge in Britain. Other stone circles and megalithic monuments also erected around this time.
c. 2,600 BC	Construction of the Great Pyramid of Giza.
428-340 BC	Life of Plato, the Greek philosopher.
c. 400 BC	Final form of the zodiac established by Babylonians.
280 BC	First school of Greek astrology founded on the island of Cos. Aristarchus of Samos proposes that the earth goes round the sun.
c. 230 BC	Eratosthenes attempts to calculate the circumference of the earth.
1st century AD	Marcus Manilius, the Roman, writes *Astronomica*.
c. AD 100	Ptolemy writes his famous work, the *Tetrabiblos*.
354-430	Life of St Augustine, who opposes astrology.
8th century	First school of Arab astrology founded in Baghdad.
9th century	Albumazar writes his astrological manuals, later to be used extensively by European astrologers.
11th century	Statute passed forbidding the British to worship the sun and the moon.
12th century	Life of Adelard of Bath, English traveller who brings back Arabic knowledge of astrology to Europe.
1186	A forthcoming conjunction of planets terrifies the astrologers, who predict catastrophe.
1214-94	Life of Roger Bacon, astrologer, scientist and alchemist.
1327	Professor of Bologna University put to death for drawing up the horoscope of Christ.
1391	Chaucer writes *A Treatise on the Astrolabe*.
1492	First astrological almanack published in England.
1493-1541	Life of Paracelsus, Swiss physician and writer who uses astrology in his work.
1543	Copernicus' treatise on the solar system published.
1554	First parody of an almanack published in England.
1577	Tycho Brahe shows that a comet lies beyond the moon's orbit.
1609	Johannes Kepler writes on the laws of planetary motion.
1616-54	Life of Nicholas Culpeper, a physician specializing in the use of herbs prescribed according to astrological principles.

1651	William Lilly prints some suggestive astrological predictions which will later be held to have forecast the Great Fire of London in 1666.
1701	Jonathan Swift plays his infamous trick on the almanack maker, Mr Partridge.
1752-1839	Life of Ebenezer Sibly, author of *The Celestial Art of Astrology*.
1776-1839	Life of Lady Hester Stanhope, an eccentric aristocrat who practises her own version of astrology.
1781	Discovery of the planet Uranus.
1791	First issue of *The Conjuror's Magazine* which contains much astrological material.
1824	Vagrancy Act passed, forbidding the practice of fortune-telling.
1826	First edition of Raphael's almanack, called then *The Prophetic Messenger*.
1835-1906	Life of Richard Garnett, Keeper of Books at the British Museum, author of a book on the relationship between the planets and mental illness.
1860-1917	Life of William Allen (Alan Leo) who publishes many popular books on astrology.
1878	Founding of the Theosophical Society.
1887-1968	Life of Charles Carter, one of the most respected modern writers on astrology.
1920	Birth of John Addey, Patron of the Astrological Association and pioneer of new techniques in astrology.
1930	First newspaper column of astrology printed.
1943	Faked copies of German astrological magazine, *Zenit*, sent to enemy territory.
1958	Founding of the Astrological Association in Britain.

Glossary

Almanack — An annual calendar, very popular in the sixteenth and seventeenth centuries. It gave much advice and prediction based on astrological lore.

Ascendant — Otherwise known as the Rising Sign. The ascendant is the sign of the zodiac that was rising above the eastern horizon at the time of birth, and is very important in a person's horoscope.

Aspect — An aspect is formed when two planets are in relationship with each other in the horoscope. According to astrological tradition, whether they are in aspect or not depends upon the number of degrees that separate them in the zodiac circle.

Astrology — The tradition of mapping the positions of the planets as seen from earth, and of interpreting the significance of these in relation to human affairs. There are different branches of astrology, the main ones being Electional (see below), Mundane (which relates to the fate and fortunes of nations), Natal (see below) and Horary (see below). Natal astrology is the most popular in the twentieth century.

Celestial/Celestial Bodies — Of the skies or heavens; all the "bodies", for example, the sun, moon, stars, etc that are visible in the skies.

Chart/Birthchart — Other terms used for the horoscope.

Comet — A comet generally looks like a star with a flaming tail, and may arrive in the solar system, either predictably or without warning. This is because although comets actually orbit the sun, some have regular orbits, which bring them into view again after a certain number of years, while others have such huge orbits that they only appear in the solar system once and are never seen again. The appearance of a comet in the sky aroused much concern and awe in times gone by.

Conjunction — The planetary aspect formed when two or more planets are close to each other in the zodiac.

Constellation — A group of fixed stars in the sky, often given a mythological name. The constellations are not the same as the signs of the zodiac, and do not play a great part in astrology.

Divination — Astrology is a form of divination, as are palmistry, card-reading, and crystal-gazing. Divination means trying to find the inner, hidden meaning, from an external pattern. Astrology uses the position of the planets as the "pattern", and is considered to be highly disciplined compared to other methods of divination, as it involves a thorough understanding of specific rules and techniques.

Eclipse — An eclipse occurs when one heavenly body moves in front of another and blocks it from our view. The eclipses which chiefly concern us are those of the sun (when the moon passes between the sun and the earth) and those of the moon (when the earth is in exact alignment between the sun and the moon and thus cuts out the rays of the sun which would normally illuminate the moon).

Ecliptic — The path which the sun apparently takes around the earth each year. In fact, it represents the path of the earth around the sun. Known in astrology as the zodiac.

Electional Astrology — The use of astrology to choose a suitable moment for beginning an enterprise.

Ephemeris — Tables of planetary positions, usually giving information for each day of the year. These are used by astrologers in calculating horoscopes.

Fixed Stars — Stars outside our solar system; they are so far away that they scarcely appear to change their position in relation to one another. Certain very conspicuous fixed stars are sometimes used in astrological interpretation, but in general they are not of great importance in astrology.

Horary Astrology — A branch of astrology concerned with the answering of questions. A question is posed, a horoscope is drawn up for the time at which the question was asked, and the astrologer endeavours to find the answer or the future from the horoscope.

Horoscope (or Nativity) — A map of the planetary positions, drawn up for the moment of birth, or of an event, and adjusted for that place at which the birth or the event occurred.

Houses — Just as the planets will be in zodiac signs in the horoscope, so will they also be in houses. The houses form another twelve-fold division of the horoscope; each house relates to a particular aspect of life — for example, the second house is money and possessions, the fourth represents the home, and so on. The houses in which the planets lie are taken into account in interpretation.

Humour — In medieval medicine man was said to be made of four humours. These were closely related to the four elements in astrology — earth, water, fire and air.

Midheaven — The degree of the zodiac which was nearest to the southernmost point of the sky at the time of birth. Said to denote a person's standing and reputation in the world.

Natal Astrology — The astrological tradition of interpreting a birth chart for an individual.

Orbit — The elliptical path which a planet takes as it travels around the sun.

Planets — In astrology, the term planets includes the sun and the moon.

Retrograde — Retrograde motion is when a planet appears to be going backwards in its orbit, as we see it from earth.

Solstice — Means when the sun stands still, and refers to the times in midsummer (around 21 June) and midwinter (21 December) when the sun reaches its most extreme positions north and south respectively. We commonly refer to the solstices as the longest and shortest days of the year.

Talisman — A lucky amulet or charm, made in accordance with the planetary forces that one wishes to invoke.

Zodiac — A division of the ecliptic into twelve equal parts, each part named after a creature — with the exception of Libra, the scales.

For a fuller explanation of the astronomical terms included here, the reader is referred to any basic book on astronomy or the solar system. Astronomy as it relates to astrology is dealt with in a special book called *The Astrologer's Astronomical Handbook* by Jeff Mayo (L.N. Fowler and Co Ltd, 1979)

Books for Further Reading

Linda Goodman,
Sun Signs,
Pan Books, 1970

Liz Greene,
Looking at Astrology,
Coventure, 1977

Warren Kenton,
Astrology, the Celestial Mirror,
Thames and Hudson, 1974

Jeff Mayo,
Teach Yourself Astrology,
Teach Yourself Books, 1964

James Murden,
Young Astronomer's Handbook,
Piccolo, 1977

A.W. Unwin,
The Calendar,
Spotlight Books, Basil Blackwell, 1976

Keith Wicks,
Stars and Planets,
New Horizon Library, Sampson Low, 1977

For Older Readers

Zolar,
The History of Astrology,
W. Foulsham and Co, 1972

Index

The numbers in **bold type** refer to the figure numbers of the illustrations

Addey, John 64; **59**
Adelard of Bath 21
Agrippa, Heinrich Cornelius 36
Albumazar 21; **19**
alchemy 37-38
almanacks 42-47, 49-50; **39, 40, 41, 42, 44**
Aquinas, Thomas 22
Arab astrologers 19, 20-21
Aristarchus 17
Aristotle 17, 21
ascendant 7; **3, 58**
aspects 12; **9**
astrolabe 28; **26**
The Astrologaster 45
The Astrologer (a comedy) 48-49
The Astrologer (a magazine) 57-59; **54**
The Astrologer of the Nineteenth Century 54-55; **50, 51**
Astrologers' Feasts 45
Astrological Association 59-61
Astrological Conference 61; **57, 58**
Astrological Lodge 57, 59
astrological magazines 54-55, 57-59
astrology (definition of) 5, 13
   and the law 40, 52-53, 63
   and magic 22, 57; **36**
   and medicine 23-24, 31-32, 37, 42; **23**
   and newspapers 59, 63
   and religion 5, 21-22, 29, 30
   and science 48, 61-63, 64
   electional 21
   horary 21, 39-42
astronomy 13, 21, 29; **30, 31**
Augustine, St. 21

Babylon 13-15
Bacon, Roger 28
Brahe, Tycho 29
Bruno, Giordano 29

Carter, Charles 59; **56**
Chaldeans 16
Chamber, John 31
Chapman, George 34
Chaucer 23, 28
comets 23, 29, 37, 42-43; **20, 35**
Complaint of Mars and Venus 28; **25**
computers 64-65
Copernicus, Nicholas 29
   Copernican system 28
cosmology, theories of 15, 17, 25, 29; **27, 28, 29**
Culpeper, Nicholas 42

decans 16
Dee, John 32-33

eclipses 14, 23; **39**
ecliptic 7; **2**
Egypt 15-16
   pyramids of 16; **15**
elements (earth, water, fire and air) 11, 23
Elizabeth I 32-33
ephemeris 7, 54
Evans, John Arise 39; **38**

Faculty of Astrological Studies 61
"fixed stars" 14, 17
Fludd, Robert 37
Forman, Simon 42
Fulke, William 30

Galen 23
Garnett, Richard 56-57; **53**
Gauquelin, Michel 64
Greece, Ancient 16-18, 19

Henry VIII 31
Herschel, William 52; **48, 49**
Heydon, Christopher 31
Hipparchus 17; **16**
Hitler, Adolf 59
horoscope 5, 6-12, 42, 48; **60**
houses (of horoscope) 40
"humours", four 23; **21**

Inferno (by Dante) 32

Jupiter 8, 28, 29, 49; **33, 34**

Kepler, Johannes 29
Krafft, Karl Ernst 59

Leo, Alan (William F. Allen) 59; **55**
Lilly, William 39-42, 45-46, 47; **37**
London, Great Fire of 45-46; **43**

Marcus Manilius 18-19
Mars 8, 28; **33**
Mayo School of Astrology 61
Mercury 8, 12, 38; **5**
Midheaven 7
moon 6, 8, 17, 20, 29; **4**

Naylor, R.H. 59
Neptune 9, 12, 52
Nostradamus 59
Nut (Egyptian goddess) 16; **13**

Order of the Golden Dawn 57

71

Paracelsus 5, 37
Partridge, John 47
planets 6, 7, 8-9, 14, 25, 52
   (*see also under individual names*)
   planetary correspondences 25, 42, 51; **24**
   planetary hours 25
   planetary orbits 7, 8, 29
Plato 17, 21
Pluto 9, 52
Ptolemy 18
   Ptolomaic system **27**

"Raphael" (Robert Cross Smith) 54
retrograde motion 8, 34

Roman astrologers 18-19
Rosicrucians 37

Saturn 9, 28; **6**
Shakespeare, William 34, 42
Sibly, Ebenezer 50; **46, 47**
solar system 7, 17, 29
Stanhope, Lady Lucy Hester 51
stone circles 20; **18**
sun 6, 8
Swift, Jonathan 47

talismans 25, 54, 55
telescope, invention of 29
Theosophical Society 57, 59

Uranus 9, 52; **49**

Vagrancy Act (1824) 52-53, 63
Venus 8, 14, 28
Vettius Valens 18

Wharton, George 45
Wohl, Louis de 59
World War, Second, 59
Worsdale, John 50

Yeats, W.B. 57

"Zadkiel" (James Morrison) 55
Zadkiel's Magazine 52
ziggurats 13; **10**
zodiac 7, 10-11, 14, 34; **1, 7, 8, 11, 14, 17, 22**